Contents

SHREK THE THIRD™

Annual 2008

DREAMWORKS™

Pedigree®

Published by Pedigree Books LTD
Beech Hill House, Walnut Gardens, Exeter, Devon EX4 4DH
books@pedigreegroup.co.uk
Published in 2007

£7.99

Meet the Characters

DONKEY

Donkey's got a mouth that just won't quit, as well as the heart of a noble steed. Having married Dragon, Shrek's best friend is now the proud father of a litter of Dronkeys. Despite wanting to spend time with his family, he will always find time to have an adventure.

SHREK

Shrek is an ogre with a heart of gold. He can't wait to escape the hectic life of the kingdom and return to his simple life in the swamp with his wife Fiona and his friends Puss and Donkey. He is about to learn that marrying a princess brings with it a certain amount of responsibility.

PUSS IN BOOTS

Shrek's other loyal sidekick, Puss In Boots, has the strength, bravery and romanticism of Zorro, but in the body of a cute little kitty-cat. Ever the ladies cat, he often gives Shrek the bachelor's point of view.

PRINCE CHARMING

Still a momma's boy at heart, Prince Charming is determined to win back his happily ever after, even if that means destroying Shrek and Fiona in the process.

ARTIE

Arthur Pendragon is Fiona's cousin and the next heir to the throne of Far Far Away.

QUEEN LILLIAN

Queen Lillian is more than a typical mother. She is an amazing leader and well trained in combat.

FIONA

Princess Fiona is not your typical damsel in distress. She's smart, tough, and has been know to dropkick a band of outlaws. She also happens to be an Ogre. Having met the love of her life, Fiona has abandoned her former fairy-tale fantasies. She inspires the other princesses to do the same, helping each one find their inner strength.

Medieval Times

Our story begins in a run down theatre in downtown Far Far Away. Lightning cracks and thunder booms. The audience gasps as a familiar looking man comes out onto the stage riding a wooden toy horse.

"Whoa there, Chauncey!" It was Prince Charming. He got off his toy horse and struck a dramatic pose. The audience giggled.

A short man in a bad ogre outfit made his way out on to the stage. "Grrrr!" growled the ogre.
"Prepare yourself foul beast!" cried Charming as he charged at the ogre with his sword drawn.
Suddenly part of the stage scenery fell over and nearly squashed the prince. The crowd erupted into laughter as Charming fumed, "You'll be sorry one day!"
Charming stormed off stage and back to his dressing room.

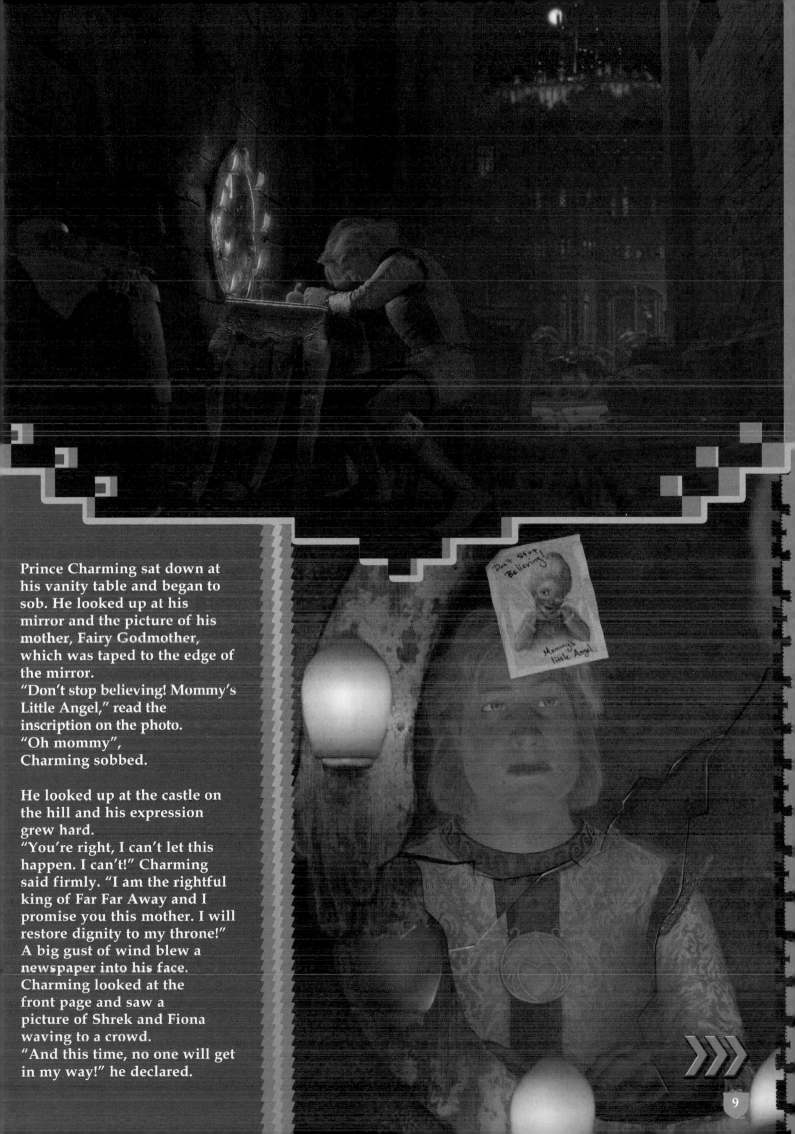

Prince Charming sat down at his vanity table and began to sob. He looked up at his mirror and the picture of his mother, Fairy Godmother, which was taped to the edge of the mirror.

"Don't stop believing! Mommy's Little Angel," read the inscription on the photo.

"Oh mommy", Charming sobbed.

He looked up at the castle on the hill and his expression grew hard.

"You're right, I can't let this happen. I can't!" Charming said firmly. "I am the rightful king of Far Far Away and I promise you this mother. I will restore dignity to my throne!" A big gust of wind blew a newspaper into his face. Charming looked at the front page and saw a picture of Shrek and Fiona waving to a crowd.

"And this time, no one will get in my way!" he declared.

Up at the castle the next morning, the sun was just breaking through the window of Shrek and Fiona's bedroom. "Good morning." Fiona said to Shrek. "Good morning." he replied. Suddenly the bedroom doors flew open and Donkey and the Dronkeys burst in. The Dronkeys flew straight over to Shrek who cowered under the bed covers.

At the Palace

"Okay. You have a very busy day filling in for the king and Queen," said Puss as he entered the bedroom. "There are several functions that require your attendance." "Oh joy!" said Shrek sarcastically trying to pull the covers back over his head. Donkey pulled the bedcovers off the bed only to reveal Shrek's bare, hairy legs. "Aaahhh! You really need to get yourself a pair of jammies!" yelled Donkey.

Shrek's first duty of the day was a knighting. A large crowd had gathered to see the brave young man who knelt nervously before Shrek. Shrek looked at Puss for direction - he had never knighted anybody before. Puss motioned how to knight a person with his sword and Shrek practiced a couple of times before walking up to the knight and accidentally stabbing him!

Next, Shrek and Fiona had to go to a launching of a ship. Shrek had the responsibility of breaking a champagne bottle on the ship for luck. Shrek leant on the boat and accidentally pushed it into the sea! He reacted quickly and threw the bottle at the boat as it floated away. Unfortunately the bottle punched a big hole in the boat and it promptly sank! Shrek turned to see the crowd all shaking their heads as they turned to leave.

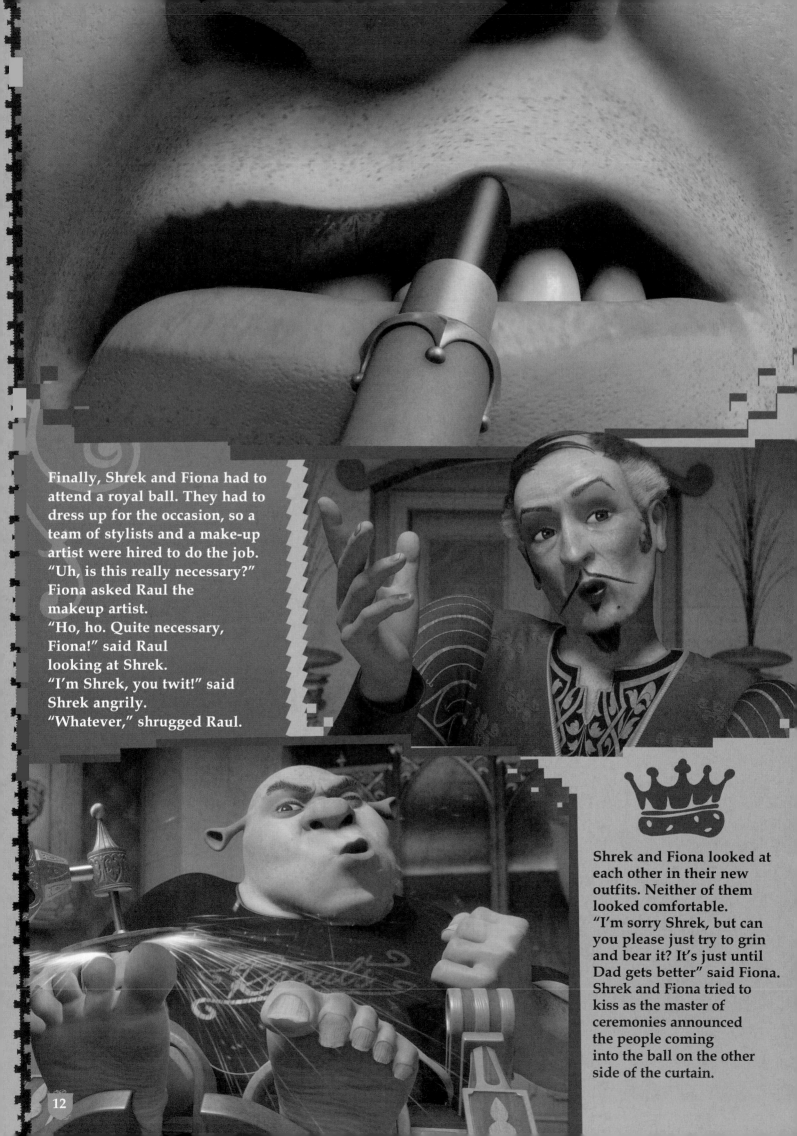

Finally, Shrek and Fiona had to attend a royal ball. They had to dress up for the occasion, so a team of stylists and a make-up artist were hired to do the job.
"Uh, is this really necessary?" Fiona asked Raul the makeup artist.
"Ho, ho. Quite necessary, Fiona!" said Raul looking at Shrek.
"I'm Shrek, you twit!" said Shrek angrily.
"Whatever," shrugged Raul.

Shrek and Fiona looked at each other in their new outfits. Neither of them looked comfortable.
"I'm sorry Shrek, but can you please just try to grin and bear it? It's just until Dad gets better" said Fiona. Shrek and Fiona tried to kiss as the master of ceremonies announced the people coming into the ball on the other side of the curtain.

"Oh, my butt is itching up a storm and I can't reach it in this monkey suit!" said Shrek desperately trying to scratch his butt. "Hey you. Come here!" he shouted to a man holding a sceptre. "What's your name?"
"Eh, Fiddlesworth, Sir."
The man replied.
"Hoo hoo. Perfect" said Shrek. Finally the master of ceremonies announced Shrek and Fiona.
"Ladies and gentlemen, Princess Fiona and Sir Shrek!"

The curtain opened to reveal Fiddlesworth scratching away at Shrek's butt.
"Scratch it, Fiddler old boy. Ahh! All right, you got it..."
"Uh, Shrek?" said Fiona.
Shrek turned around to see the entire ballroom staring at him. Suddenly his belt buckle popped off and hit Donkey in the eye. Donkey stumbled into the crowd knocking over vases and sending water everywhere. Fiona slipped in the water and landed in a crumpled heap on the stage. It was a disaster!

Later that night, Shrek and Fiona returned to their room in the castle.
"That's it we are leaving!" yelled Shrek as he wiped off his makeup and pulled off his wig.
"Honey, please calm down" said Fiona "Just think… a couple more days, and we'll be back home in our vermin-filled shack, strewn with fungus, filled with the rotting stench of mud and neglect."
Shrek smiled "You had me at 'vermin-filled.'"

"And, uh… maybe even the pitter-patter of little feet on the floor…?" started Fiona.
"Donkey?" asked Shrek.
"No Shrek, um…what if they were little ogre feet?" said Fiona.
Shrek jumped off the bed and fell to the floor in shock. He picked himself up and looked at Fiona.

"Honey? Let's try and be rational about this. Have you seen a baby lately? They just eat and poop and they cry and then they cry when they poop 'n they poop when they cry and they…"Shrek said.
"Shrek," said Fiona interrupting, "don't you ever think about having a family?"
"Right now," answered Shrek as he took Fiona's hand, "you're my family."

Fiona looked a little disappointed and was abut to say something when there was a loud knock at the door. The door burst open to reveal a Royal Page looking very serious.
Shrek sprang to his feet at the interruption "Well, somebody better be dying" shouted Shrek.

SHREK CROSSWORD

ACROSS
1 He only has one eye.
3 If he lies his nose will grow.
5 What do you get if you cross a Dragon and a Donkey
8 He's married to a dragon.
9 He's a very froggy king.
10 His mommy was Fairy Godmother.

DOWN
2 The love of Shrek's life.
4 Arties surname.
6 Everybody's favourite wizard.
7 He's a big green ogre.

ARTIE
CHARMING
DONKEY
DRAGON
DRONKEY

FIONA
KING
LILLIAN
MERLIN

MICE
PIG
PINOCCHIO
PUSS
SHREK

G	F	G	G	G	Y	C	O	X	N	Y	G	L	U	N
Y	A	I	H	I	R	H	Q	D	D	I	I	I	O	F
E	S	P	O	Q	Q	A	L	X	O	L	L	G	K	W
K	Y	E	K	N	O	R	D	W	L	F	A	R	C	C
N	E	C	I	M	A	M	Q	I	A	R	P	T	E	A
O	E	M	P	D	O	I	A	T	D	U	M	B	G	M
D	K	P	C	I	P	N	O	V	S	I	D	H	S	S
L	H	I	T	C	N	G	S	S	Z	H	N	Y	E	G
A	Z	P	H	T	D	O	I	W	F	N	A	G	N	I
R	V	G	Q	I	I	U	C	A	R	S	H	R	E	K
T	H	H	N	Q	T	K	I	C	T	A	A	J	I	P
I	S	E	H	I	S	P	C	X	H	P	S	O	M	P
E	X	O	B	M	K	U	V	U	X	I	Z	Z	D	L
T	Y	S	M	P	S	Y	R	K	C	K	O	N	R	I
B	A	Z	B	A	Z	W	J	J	F	S	R	H	C	B

SHREK
WORD SEARCH

The King is Dead!

Shrek and Fiona dashed to King Harold's bedroom where Queen Lillian was waiting.
"I'm dying" said King Harold.

"Harold!" exclaimed the Queen. "Don't forget to pay the gardener, Lillian," the king reminded her.
"Of course darling," the Queen replied.
"Fiona," the king said horsley, "I know I have made many mistakes with you but your love for Shrek has taught me so much."
Fiona smiled at her father as he motioned to Shrek to come closer.

"My dear boy, I am proud to call you my son." King Harold said to Shrek.
"And I am proud to call you my Frog...King Dad in-law."
Shrek replied.
"Shrek, please come closer," the king whispered, "This kingdom needs a new king. You and Fiona are next in line for the throne."

"Ooo. Next in line." Shrek said nervously, "Now you see Dad, that's why people love you. Even on your deathbed you're still making jokes!"

The king just stared at Shrek, stone faced. Shrek bent down closer to the king.

"Oh come on Dad...an ogre as king? I don't think that's such a good idea. There's got to be somebody else. Anybody?" Shrek asked desperately.

"Aside from you, there is only one remaining heir," the king breathlessly replied.

"Really!? Who is he, Dad? What's his name?" asked Shrek.

"His name is...is...is..." the king stammered, "his name is Arthur."

"Arthur?" asked Shrek.

"I know you'll do what's...riiiight..."

With that, King Harold took his last breath. The king was dead.

"Harold!?" cried the Queen.

Fiona burst into tears and hugged Shrek. Puss took of his hat and hung his head respectfully. No one could quite believe that the king was gone. They were all in shock.

Later that night, Prince Charming arrived at the Poison Apple. As he walked inside, smoke wafted across the room while a wicked witch played the piano. The bar was filled with fairy-tale villains.

Charming made his way over to the bar tender, cleared his throat and said "What does a prince have to do to get a drink around here?"

Charming's New Friends

Mabel, one of the ugly stepsisters turned to Charming and glared at him.
"Ah Mabel, why they call you an ugly stepsister I'll never know" said Charming as he winked at her.
"What do you want, Charming?" asked Mabel gruffly.
"Oh not much, just a chance at redemption..." Charming chuckled, "and a Fuzzy Navel" he continued as he turned to the bar. "And Fuzzy Navels for all my friends!"

The fairy-tale villains again stopped what they were doing.
"We're not your friends!" yelled Captain Hook as the villains moved menacingly towards Charming.

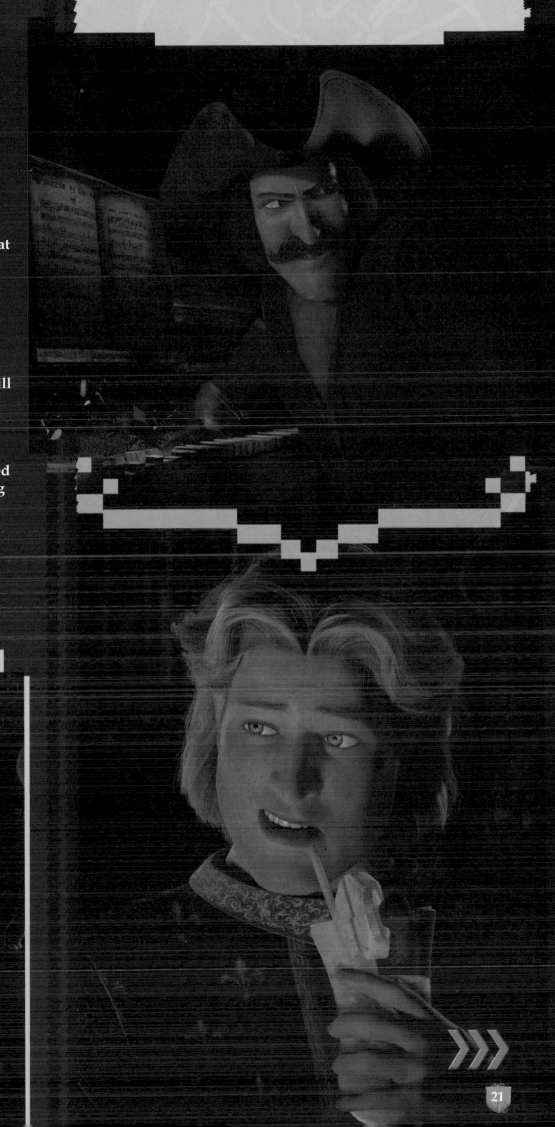

Mabel grabbed Charming and pinned him to the bar.
"You don't belong here!" growled Captain Hook.
"You're right! Oh, I mean you're absolutely right, but I mean, do any of us?" Charming replied.
"Do a number on his face!" shouted Cyclops.
"No, no, wait, wait, wait! We are more alike than you think. Once upon a time, someone decided that we were the losers. But there are two sides to ever story. And our story has not been told!" yelped Charming.

The bar full of rag-tag villains were beginning to listen so Charming continued, "So who will join me? Who wants to come out on top for once? Who wants their happily ever after?"
The crowd of villains began to clap and cheer. Soon things started to get a bit rowdy and before long a full-scale bar room brawl had broken out. Charming looked on, smiling to himself and sipping from his Fuzzy Navel.

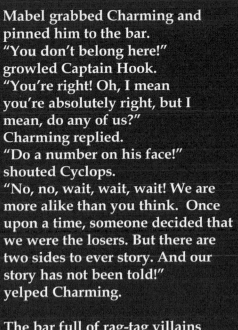

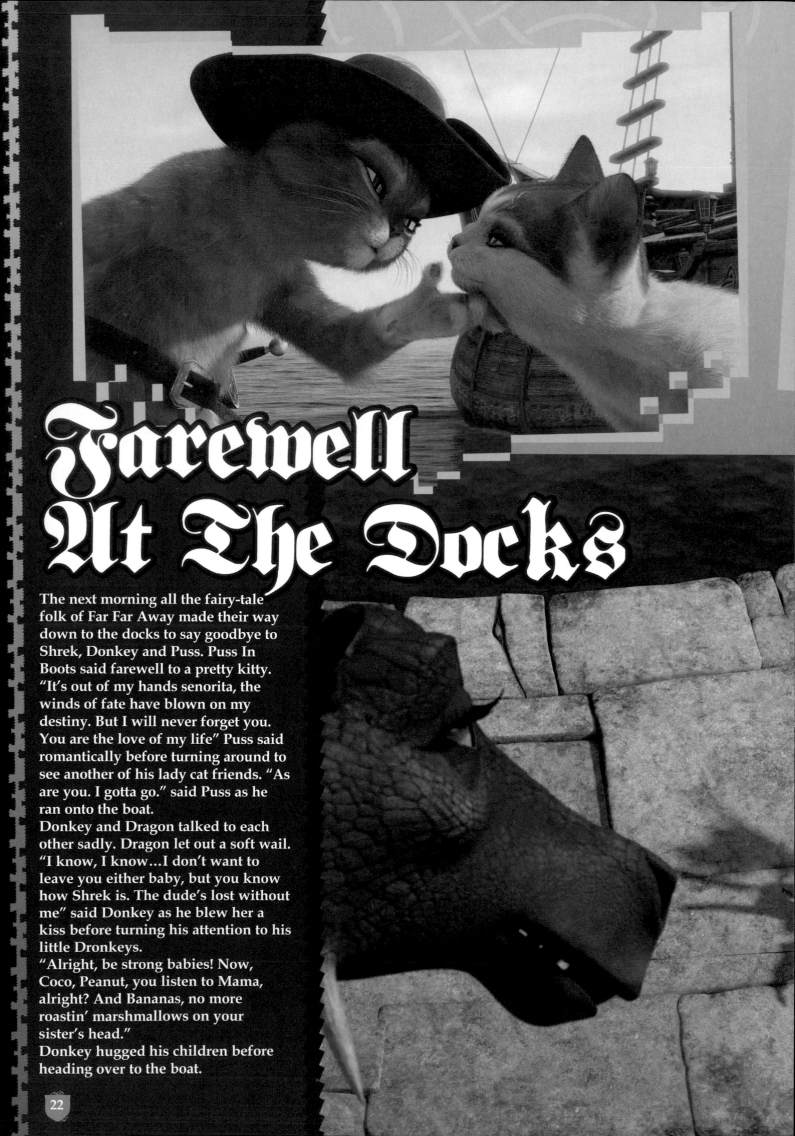

Farewell At The Docks

The next morning all the fairy-tale folk of Far Far Away made their way down to the docks to say goodbye to Shrek, Donkey and Puss. Puss In Boots said farewell to a pretty kitty. "It's out of my hands senorita, the winds of fate have blown on my destiny. But I will never forget you. You are the love of my life" Puss said romantically before turning around to see another of his lady cat friends. "As are you. I gotta go." said Puss as he ran onto the boat.

Donkey and Dragon talked to each other sadly. Dragon let out a soft wail. "I know, I know…I don't want to leave you either baby, but you know how Shrek is. The dude's lost without me" said Donkey as he blew her a kiss before turning his attention to his little Dronkeys.

"Alright, be strong babies! Now, Coco, Peanut, you listen to Mama, alright? And Bananas, no more roastin' marshmallows on your sister's head."

Donkey hugged his children before heading over to the boat.

Shrek made his way over to Fiona to say goodbye.

"Shrek," said Fiona, "there's something I have to tell you."

"I know. Your mother was hoping we'd stay, but c'mon, Far Far Away will be a much safer place without me in charge" replied Shrek.

"It's not that. No. It's, you see...I just really wish you weren't leaving right now because..." said Fiona before Shrek interrupted her.

"Ah, me too, but trust me, your cousin Arthur is gonna be a great king. And if he gives me any trouble, I've always got persuasion and reason. Here's persuasion," he said holding up his right fist, "and here's reason," said Shrek holding up his left fist and chuckling.

Fiona just stared at Shrek.

"Fiona, soon it's just going to be you and me and our swamp," said Shrek.

"It's not just going to be you and me" Fiona said hesitantly.

"All aboard," yelled the ships captain.

Shrek kissed Fiona and ran to the ship.

"It will be. I promise. I love you," Shrek cried as he climbed on board.

"Shrek!" yelled Fiona

"Yeah. What is it?" Shrek yelled back.

"I'm pregnant! You're going to be a father!"

"That's great" yelled Shrek with a nervous laugh.

"I'm glad you think so! I love you" Fiona shouted as the ship sailed away and out to sea.

»»»

Copy the Colours

24

Shrek and the gang love to spend time together, as you can see in this picture. Try and copy the colours or give it your own twist!

Worcestershire

Worcestershire Academy

Shrek, Donkey and Puss In Boots, finally arrived at the Worcestershire Academy. Worcestershire Academy was a very impressive looking place. A huge castle loomed up in front of Shrek and his friends.

"Wor-ces-ter-shireeee." said Donkey, "Now that sounds fancy."
"It's Worcestershire," replied Shrek.
"Like the Sauce!? Mmmm..." said Donkey licking his lips.

The drawbridge to the castle began to lower.
"Oohh! They must be expecting us." said Donkey.

Just then, a huge school carriage came flying up behind the intrepid trio almost hitting them. All the children at the back of the bus saw Shrek and began to scream.

"What in the shista-shire kind of place is this?" asked Donkey.
"Well," said Shrek with a concerned look on his face, "my stomach aches and my palms just got sweaty. Must be a high school."
"High school?!" cried Donkey

Shrek, Donkey and Puss continued into the school looking for Arthur.
"I'm already starting to feel nauseous from memories of wedgies and swirlies!" said Donkey nervously.
"But how did you receive the wedgies when you are clearly not the wearer of the underpants?" asked Puss.
"Let's just say some things are better left unsaid and leave it at that," replied Donkey.

The three continued into the school and came upon two geeky kids playing a role-playing board game.
"Yes! I just altered my character level to plus three superbability" said Gary.
"Hi" said Shrek interrupting the game, "we're looking for someone named…"
"Gee, who rolled a plus nine "dork" spell and summoned the beast and his quadrupeds?" asked Gary laughing with his friend.
"I know you're busy "not fitting in," Shrek continued, "but can either of you tell me where I can find Arthur?"
Gary pointed over to the jousting field and said "He's over there."

In the distance Shrek could see a brave looking knight atop a noble steed. Shrek, Donkey and Puss ran over to the field to see the jousting match.
The knight reared up on his horse and galloped down the field towards his opponent. The knight hit his opponent squarely in the chest with his lance, sending the poor kid high into the air before landing in a crumpled heap with an unceremonious thud!
The knight took off his helmet to reveal a strong and handsome face. Shrek looked on as the knight celebrated his victory with his friends.
Shrek turned to Puss, "Strong, handsome, face of a leader. Does Arthur look like a king or what?" Shrek said as he walked over to the knight.

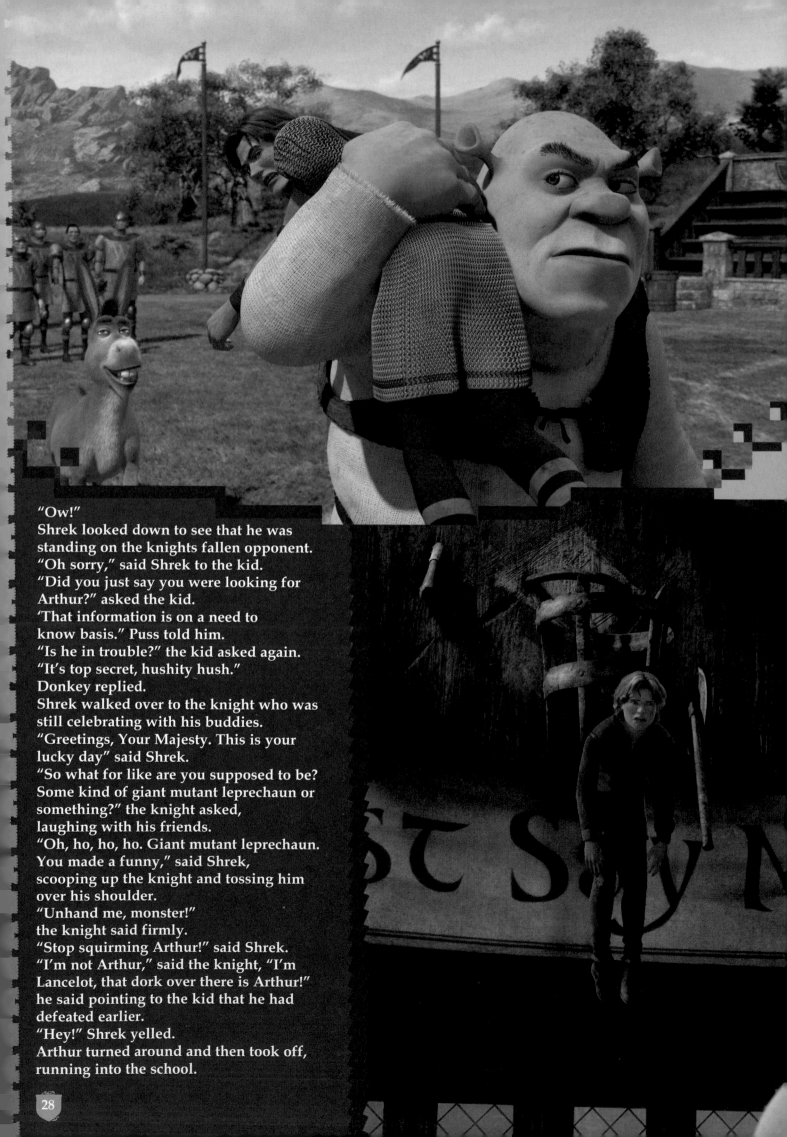

"Ow!"

Shrek looked down to see that he was standing on the knights fallen opponent.

"Oh sorry," said Shrek to the kid.

"Did you just say you were looking for Arthur?" asked the kid.

'That information is on a need to know basis." Puss told him.

"Is he in trouble?" the kid asked again.

"It's top secret, hushity hush." Donkey replied.

Shrek walked over to the knight who was still celebrating with his buddies.

"Greetings, Your Majesty. This is your lucky day" said Shrek.

"So what for like are you supposed to be? Some kind of giant mutant leprechaun or something?" the knight asked, laughing with his friends.

"Oh, ho, ho, ho. Giant mutant leprechaun. You made a funny," said Shrek, scooping up the knight and tossing him over his shoulder.

"Unhand me, monster!" the knight said firmly.

"Stop squirming Arthur!" said Shrek.

"I'm not Arthur," said the knight, "I'm Lancelot, that dork over there is Arthur!" he said pointing to the kid that he had defeated earlier.

"Hey!" Shrek yelled.

Arthur turned around and then took off, running into the school.

Shrek and Puss were walking through the corridors of the school looking for Arthur.
"Oh Arthur! Come out come out wherever you are…" yelled Shrek.
From somewhere behind them, Shrek and Puss heard a strange noise.
Suddenly, Donkey burst out of a school locker!
"Yeah, you better run you little punk no good-niks, 'cause the days of "Little Donkey Dumpy Drawers" are over!"
Donkey turned to Shrek and Puss revealing that someone had stuck a sign to his back saying "I Suck-eth".

Shrek spotted some students heading into the assembly hall and figured it would be a good place to look for Arthur. Inside the hall, Principal Pynchley was speaking to the school.
"Thank you to Professor Primbottom for his invigorating lecture on how to just say "Nay". And now without further ado, let's give a warm Worcestershier-hoozah to the winner of our "New Mascot" contest…the"
Before Principal Pynchley could finish his sentence Shrek burst through the doors of the hall.
The pupils started to clap. They all thought that Shrek had won the contest!
"Thanks so much, "said Shrek lifting his arms to silence the crowd, "let's win the big game against the visitors. Now, where's Arthur Pendragon. Some of the class started to snicker and pointed to behind Shrek.
Arthur was hanging by the mother of all wedgies on the basketball hoop.

"Hi there," said Shrek looking up at Artie, "Remember me? You mind coming down 'cause we need to get going. You're the new king of Far Far Away."

"Artie a king?" cried Lancelot, "More like the "Mayor of Loserville!"

All the students burst out laughing.

"Is this for real?" asked Artie as Puss cut him down from the basketball hoop.

"Yep", replied Shrek, "let's go get you fitted for your crown."

Artie couldn't believe his luck.

"Just give me a second." Artie said to Shrek.

"Well, well, well. Look who's a king. Farewell Lance. Hey if there's any justice in the world, next time I run into you, you'll be manager of Friars Fat Boy!"

Artie turned to Guinevere.

"Oh Gwen, I've always loved you."

Gwen looked grossed out.

"Well good friends, it breaks my heart, but I gotta go. Enjoy your stay here in prison while I rule the free world!" Artie continued.

"Alright, let's not overdo it" said Shrek trying to calm Artie down.

"I'm building my city people! Building it on rock and roll!" yelled Artie.

"You just overdid it!" grumbled Shrek as he grabbed Artie by the arm and led him out of the hall.

Charmings Coup

Meanwhile, back in Far Far Away, all the princesses and fairy-tale creatures had gathered at the castle for Fiona's baby shower. A flock of little birds gently placed a flower wreath on Fiona's head as the other princess gazed at her.

"You look darling!" exclaimed Snow White, "It's present time!"

"Oh Fiona, won't you please open mine first? It's the one in front," begged Cinderella.

Fiona read the card.

"Congratulations on your new mess maker, hopefully this helps. Love Cinderella." Fiona smiled as she opened the parcel and pulled out a pooper-scooper!

Fiona turned to another present. "Who's this one from?" she asked.

"I got you the biggest one because I love you the most!" replied Snow White while the other girls scowled at her.

Fiona unwrapped the box and out popped one of Snow Whites dwarfs.

"Um…what is it?" Fiona asked.

"Ha, haaa! He's a live-in baby-sitter." explained Snow White.

"So what are Shrek and I supposed to do?" asked Fiona.

"Well now you'll have plenty of time to work on your marriage," Rapunzel said.

"What's that supposed to mean?" asked Fiona

"Oh, come on now Fiona. You know what happens!" Rapunzel replied.

"Huh?" Sleeping Beauty said as she woke up, "You're tired all the time…"

"You'll start letting yourself go…" chimed Snow White.

"Stretch marks!" Gingerbread Man added.

"Um sorry…but how many of you have kids?" asked Fiona.

"She's right," said Doris as she squeezed herself onto the sofa, "a baby is only going to strengthen the love that Shrek and Fiona have. How did Shrek react when you told him? Tell me!"

"Oh, Shrek?" Fiona said as she laughed nervously, "Oh, well, he was uh, very um…"

Unbeknownst to Fiona and the princesses, in the skies above Far Far Away the fairy-tale villains were amassing a huge army in preparation to attack the city. Hundreds of the evil creatures were riding towards the city on broomsticks. Charming was riding side saddle with a particularly ugly witch. "Onward my new friends," he yelled "to our happily ever afters! Ha ha ha ha ha!" Just then a bug flew into his mouth! "Gaa!" Charming choked as he spat the bug out, " Now, bombs away!"

The evil trees dropped like bombs and then opened their canopies and floated down to the ground. The witches flew through the streets knocking over market stalls and sending people diving out of their way!

The pirates laughed as they vandalised carriages on the street and the evil dwarves graffiti'd shop fronts. An evil knight scared all the customers out of the coffee shop and then sat down to drink their unfinished drinks. Cyclops broke into a post box and ripped the stamps of all the letter before putting them back into the box.

"Ha, ha, ha, ha!" he laughed.

"Alright! Enough pillaging!" yelled Charming " Now we take the castle!"

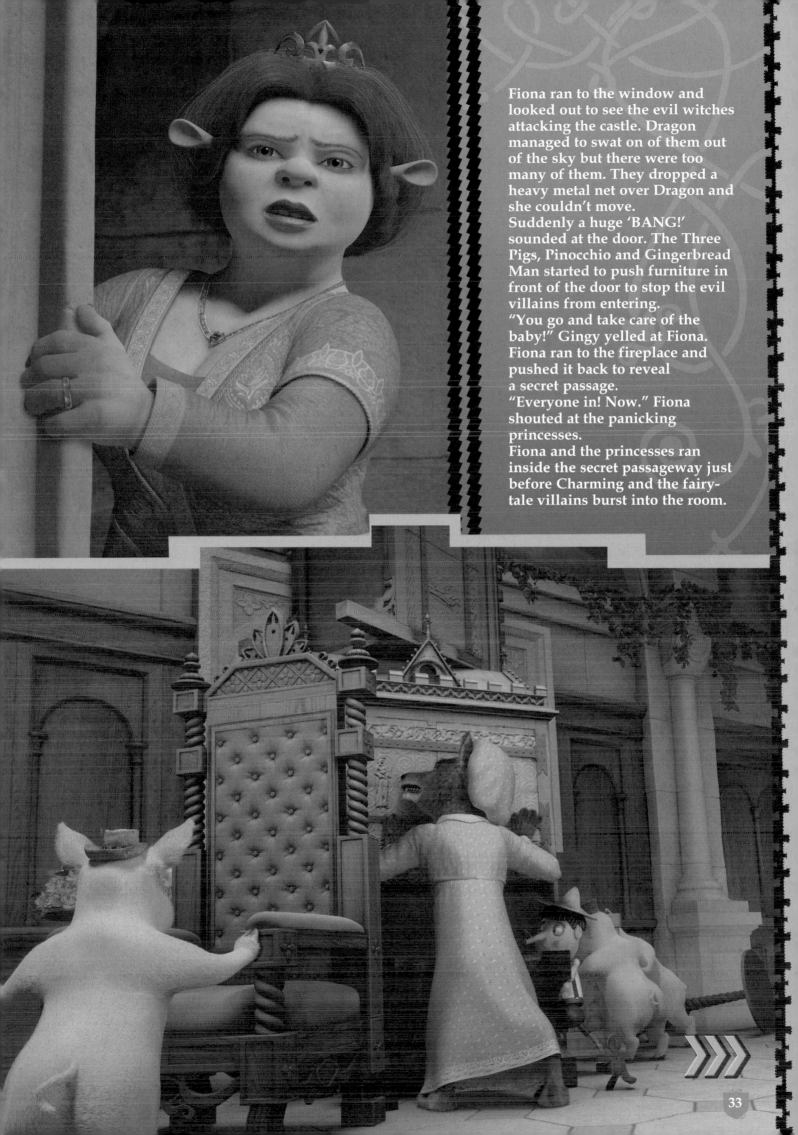

Fiona ran to the window and looked out to see the evil witches attacking the castle. Dragon managed to swat on of them out of the sky but there were too many of them. They dropped a heavy metal net over Dragon and she couldn't move.

Suddenly a huge 'BANG!' sounded at the door. The Three Pigs, Pinocchio and Gingerbread Man started to push furniture in front of the door to stop the evil villains from entering.

"You go and take care of the baby!" Gingy yelled at Fiona. Fiona ran to the fireplace and pushed it back to reveal a secret passage.

"Everyone in! Now." Fiona shouted at the panicking princesses.

Fiona and the princesses ran inside the secret passageway just before Charming and the fairy-tale villains burst into the room.

"Where are Shrek and Fiona?" demanded Prince Charming.

"Name doesn't ring a bell!" replied Gingy sarcastically.

"Yah!" agreed one of the pigs, "No bell!"

"I suggest that you freaks cooperate with the new king of Far Far Away!" said Charming angrily.

"The only thing you're ever going to be king of is "King of the Stupids!" Gingerbread Man said defiantly.

"Hook!" Charming yelled as he clicked his fingers.

Captain Hook walked over to Gingerbread Man and raised his hook under Gingy's chin.

"Start talking!" Hook growled.

Gingerbread Man tried to be strong but he was terrified! His whole live flashed before his eyes, right from when he was first baked to when Lord Farquaad pulled of his legs.

Charming was starting to get frustrated. He grabbed Pinocchio and turned him around .

"You! You can't lie. So tell me puppet…Where is Shrek?!"

Pinocchio thought for a second and then nervously said, "Well, I don't know where he's not."

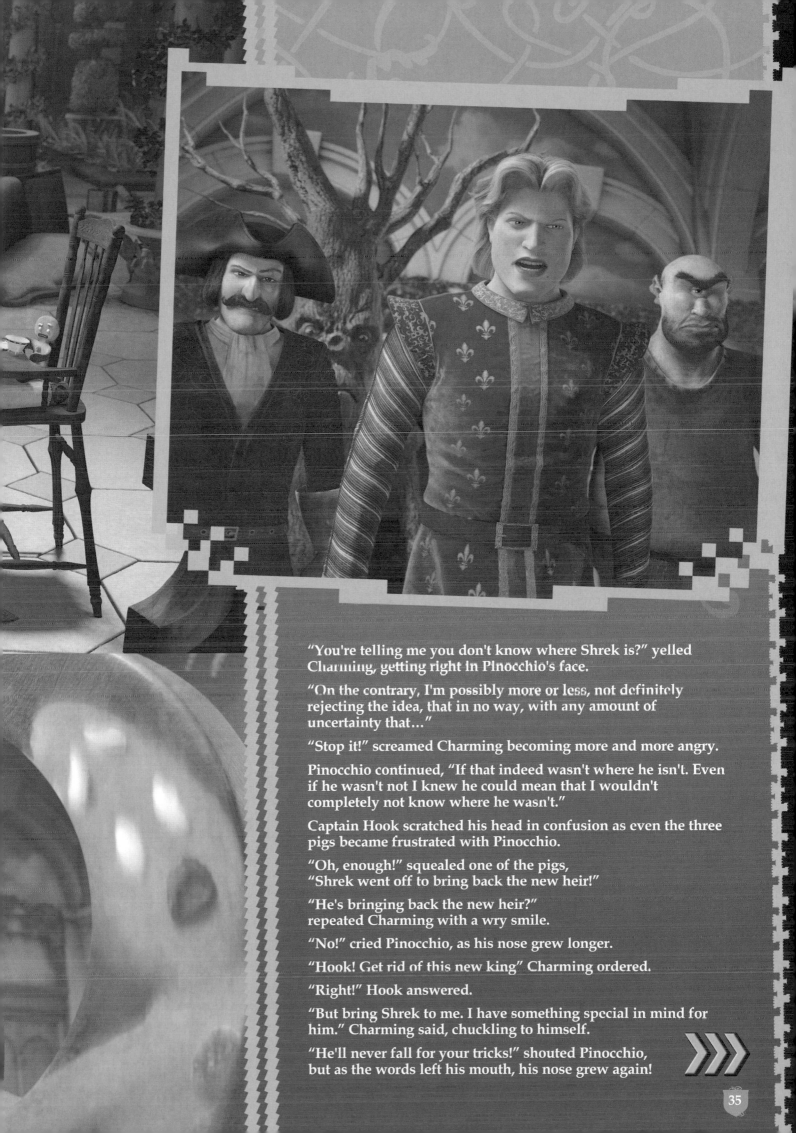

"You're telling me you don't know where Shrek is?" yelled Charming, getting right in Pinocchio's face.

"On the contrary, I'm possibly more or less, not definitely rejecting the idea, that in no way, with any amount of uncertainty that..."

"Stop it!" screamed Charming becoming more and more angry.

Pinocchio continued, "If that indeed wasn't where he isn't. Even if he wasn't not I knew he could mean that I wouldn't completely not know where he wasn't."

Captain Hook scratched his head in confusion as even the three pigs became frustrated with Pinocchio.

"Oh, enough!" squealed one of the pigs, "Shrek went off to bring back the new heir!"

"He's bringing back the new heir?" repeated Charming with a wry smile.

"No!" cried Pinocchio, as his nose grew longer.

"Hook! Get rid of this new king" Charming ordered.

"Right!" Hook answered.

"But bring Shrek to me. I have something special in mind for him." Charming said, chuckling to himself.

"He'll never fall for your tricks!" shouted Pinocchio, but as the words left his mouth, his nose grew again!

Shrek's Secret

Shrek has a disgusting secret that he doesn't want anyone to know. Can you work out from the code below just what his revolting revelation is? Look at the big picture and work out which letter relates to each picture.

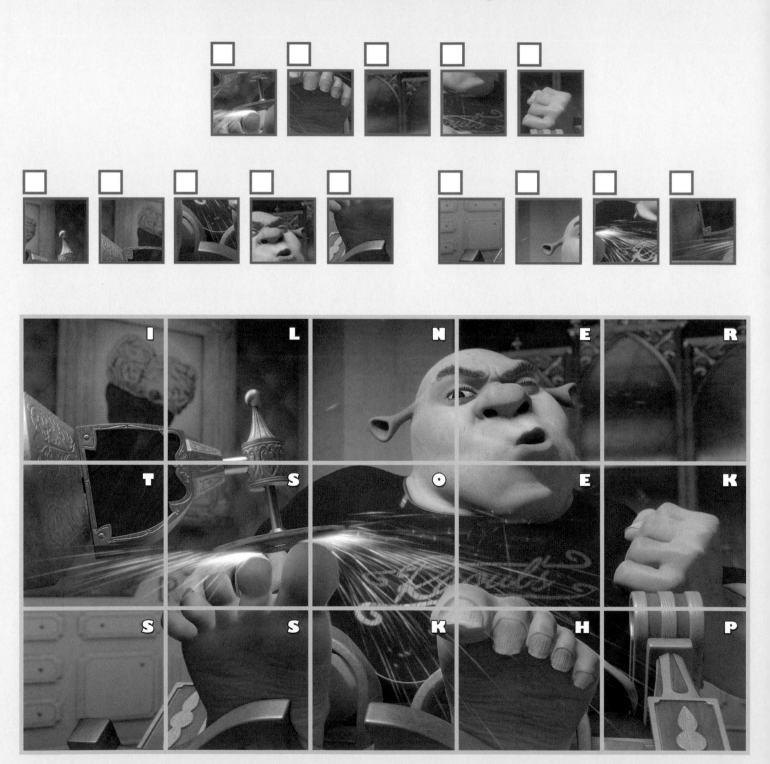

Fairy-tale Squares

This is a game for two or more players. Each player in turn draws a single line connecting two dots. The aim is to complete as many squares as possible. When you complete a square, put your initials in it. Score 1 point for each blank square and 2 points for a bonus square. If you photocopy this page, you can play the game over and over again.

Shipwreck

Back at Worcestershire Academy, Shrek, Puss, Donkey and Artie had boarded the ship and were now cutting across the open sea.

"This is going to be great! Thanks for getting me out of there Shrek. It is Shrek, right?" asked Artie.

"Anyway, that place was a dead end. But this? Whoo!! It's gonna be huge. Parties, princesses, castles. Look, I know it's not all fun and games. I'm sure I'll have to knight a few heroes, launch a ship or two?"

"Just make sure you hit the boat just right with the bottle," said Shrek thinking back to the time he had had to launch a ship.

"Boat with a bottle?" pondered Artie,
"Any idiot can hit a boat with a bottle."

Artie wandered over to the railing and looked out to sea.

"But seriously… me a king? I knew I came from royalty and all, but I just figured everyone forgot about me. Am I really the only heir?"

"The one and only," replied Shrek. "In fact the king asked for you personally."

"You'll be living in the lap of luxury." Donkey chimed in. "They got the finest chefs around waiting for you to place your order."

"And fortunately you'll have the royal food tasters," said Puss.

"Oh yeah? What do they do?" asked Artie.

"They taste the food before the king eats, to make sure it's not poisoned!" Puss told him.

"Poisoned?" chocked Artie.

"Don't worry about it, you'll be safe and sound with the help of your bodyguards!" said Donkey reassuringly.

"What?" gasped Artie, who was growing increasingly concerned.

"Indeed, you will bask in the affection of all your subjects." continued Puss.

"Just make sure they don't die of famine" said Donkey.

"Or plague" added Puss. "The coughing, the groaning, the festering sores."

"Oh! Festering sores!" Shrek interrupted, "Hey you are one funny kitty cat. We don't want Artie here getting the wrong idea."

Suddenly the boat pitched to one side. Shrek grabbed onto the railing as Donkey and Puss slid by him. He looked around for Artie, but he had gone. Artie had grabbed the wheel of the ship and was desperately spinning it, trying to turn the ship around.
"What are you doing?" yelled Shrek at Artie as he grabbed the wheel and spun it the other way.
"What does it look like?" Artie yelled right back at Shrek spinning the wheel back in the other direction.
"This really isn't up to you!" shouted Shrek as he wrestled to control the ship.
"But I don't know anything about being king" Artie shouted.
"You'll learn on the job!" yelled Shrek as Donkey and Puss rolled across the deck.

"Sorry to disappoint you, but I'm going back!" insisted Artie.
"Back to what? Being a loser?" growled Shrek.
As soon as the words had left his mouth, Shrek knew he had gone to far. Stung, Artie let go of the wheel leaving Shrek to yank hard on it. The wheel snapped from its column and nearly sent Shrek flying.
"Now look what you did!" exclaimed Shrek.
Donkey was now feeling sea-sick from all the motion and went over to the railing but as he leaned over he saw jagged rocks right in front of them.
"Shrek!" he yelled, but it was too late. The ship crashed into the rocks and everyone was flung forward.
"Land ho!" yelled the woozy ship's captain.

Meet Merlin

Shrek pulled himself up the beach carrying Donkey and Puss with him. He glared at Artie.

"Oh, nice going, Your Highness."

"Oh, so now it's "Your Highness?" What happened to "Loser?" Huh?" Artie yelled back at Shrek.

"Hey, if you think this is getting you out of anything, well it isn't. We're heading back to Far Far Away one way or another, and you're gonna be a father!" bellowed Shrek.

"A-hem" coughed Donkey, "You just said father..."

"You're...I said king. You're going to be king!" said Shrek trying to cover his tracks.

Artie marched off towards the woods.

"Where do you think you're going?" shouted Shrek.

"Far Far Away...from you!" Artie yelled back as he stormed off.

Shrek, Puss and Donkey followed Artie into the woods, trying to catch up with him.

Shrek finally caught up with Artie and decided he would try a different approach with the kid.

"Listen Artie..." said Shrek, walking behind Arthur, " If you think this whole mad scene ain't dope, I feel you dude. I mean, I'm not trying to get up in your grill or raise your roof or whatever, but what I am screaming is, yo, check out this kazing thazing bazby".

Puss and Donkey looked at each other, not believing what they were hearing.

Artie noticed a cottage off in the distance and started heading towards it. Shrek followed.

"I mean, if it doesn't groove or what I'm saying ain't straight trippin', just say, oh no you didn't, you know, you're getting' on my last nerve. And then I'll know it's...then I'll know it's whack!"

In response Artie walked past a branch in the woods and nonchalantly whacked it into Shrek's face.

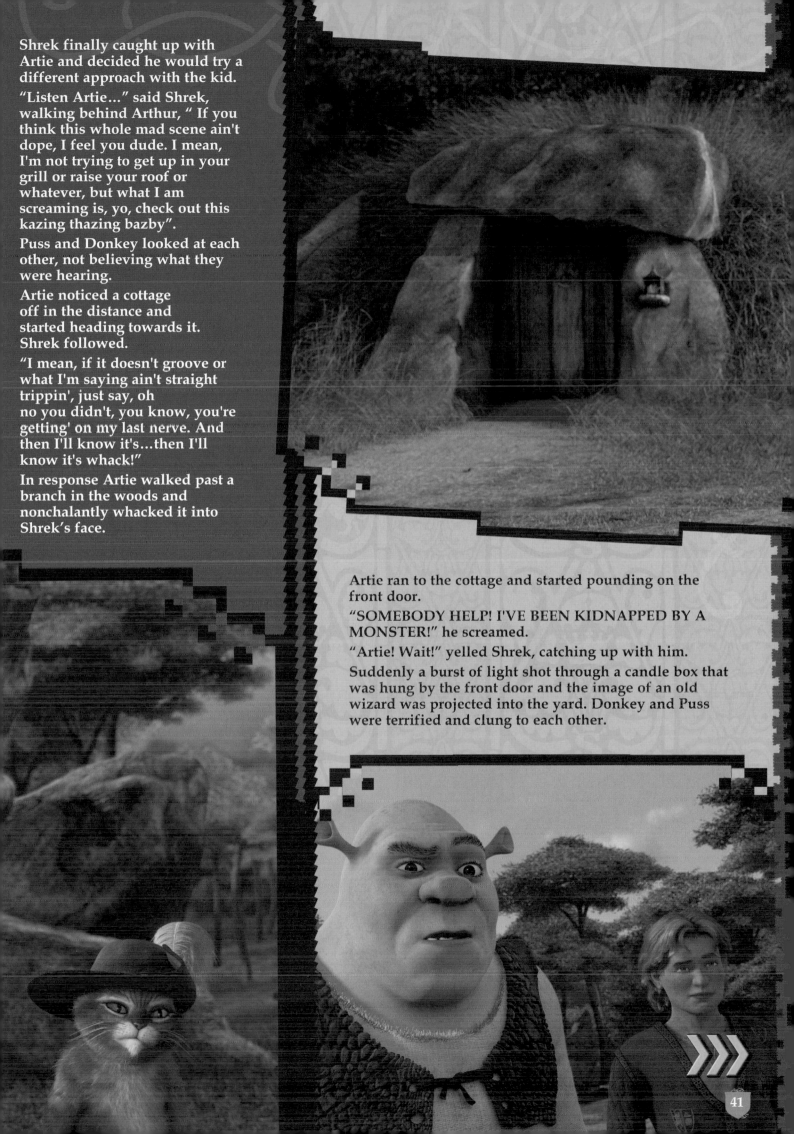

Artie ran to the cottage and started pounding on the front door.

"SOMEBODY HELP! I'VE BEEN KIDNAPPED BY A MONSTER!" he screamed.

"Artie! Wait!" yelled Shrek, catching up with him.

Suddenly a burst of light shot through a candle box that was hung by the front door and the image of an old wizard was projected into the yard. Donkey and Puss were terrified and clung to each other.

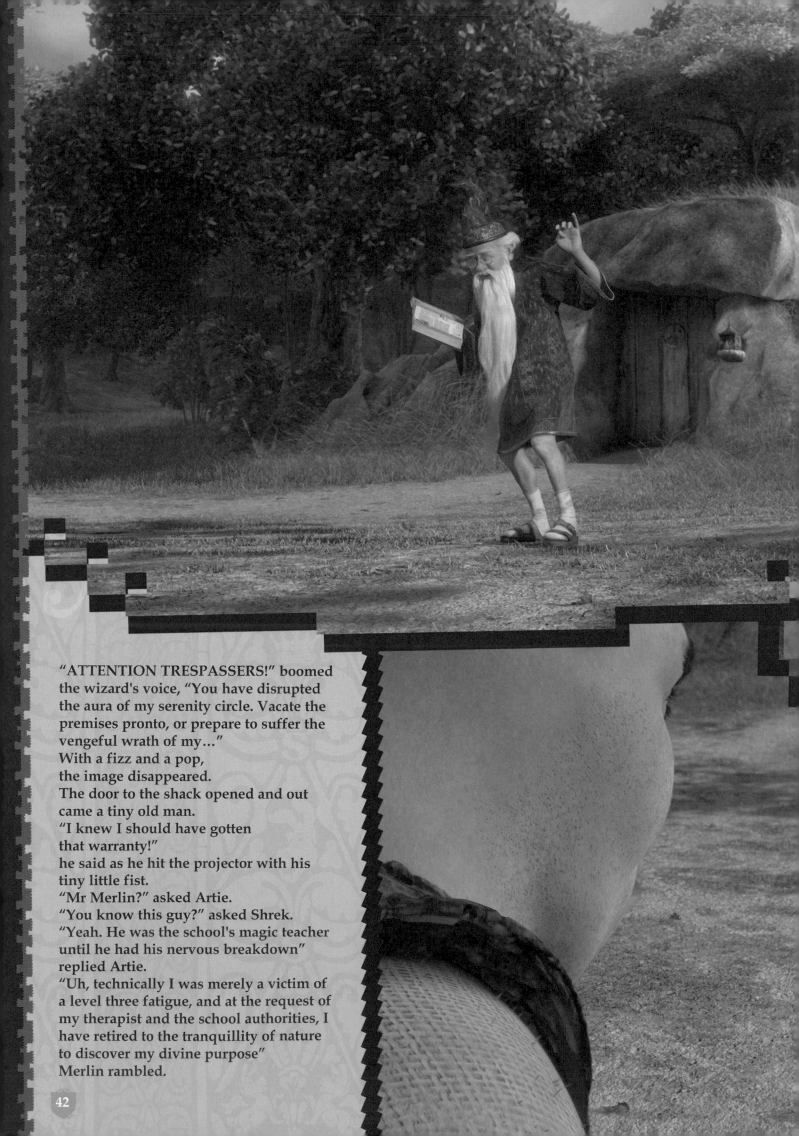

"ATTENTION TRESPASSERS!" boomed the wizard's voice, "You have disrupted the aura of my serenity circle. Vacate the premises pronto, or prepare to suffer the vengeful wrath of my…"
With a fizz and a pop,
the image disappeared.
The door to the shack opened and out came a tiny old man.
"I knew I should have gotten that warranty!"
he said as he hit the projector with his tiny little fist.
"Mr Merlin?" asked Artie.
"You know this guy?" asked Shrek.
"Yeah. He was the school's magic teacher until he had his nervous breakdown" replied Artie.
"Uh, technically I was merely a victim of a level three fatigue, and at the request of my therapist and the school authorities, I have retired to the tranquillity of nature to discover my divine purpose"
Merlin rambled.

"Would you like to try my famous rock au-gratin?" asked Merlin holding up a tray of rocks to Shrek, "It's organic!'

"Thanks, but no thanks, we've got a lot of ground to cover."

Shrek grabbed Artie by the arm and turned to leave.

"Who said I was going with you?" asked Arte pulling away from Shrek.

"Hey, understand this kid. It's no more Mr. Nice Guy from here on out!" yelled Shrek.

"Oh, so that was your "Mr. Nice Guy?" Artie mocked.

"I know, and I'm going to miss him," said Shrek.

"You know what?" yelled Artie, "Why don't you go and terrorise a village and leave me alone?"

"Uh! All your blocked denial and renunciation is rashing me up. Look! Look at that!" Merlin said as he lifted up his robe, revealing that he had broken out into a rash.

"Dios Mio!" cried Puss at the sight.

"You're not going to get anywhere unless you learn to confront your inner demons," said Merlin.

"I'd rather you just gave us directions out of here" snapped Shrek.

"I'll give you directions for that journey, but only after you take the journey to your soul" said Merlin.

"Yeah, I don't think so" said Shrek dismissively.

"Look pal, it's either that or some primal scream therapy" said Merlin before opening his mouth and starting to scream. Shrek grabbed Merlin's mouth and shut it before he could really get going.

"Alright, fine." Shrek muttered.

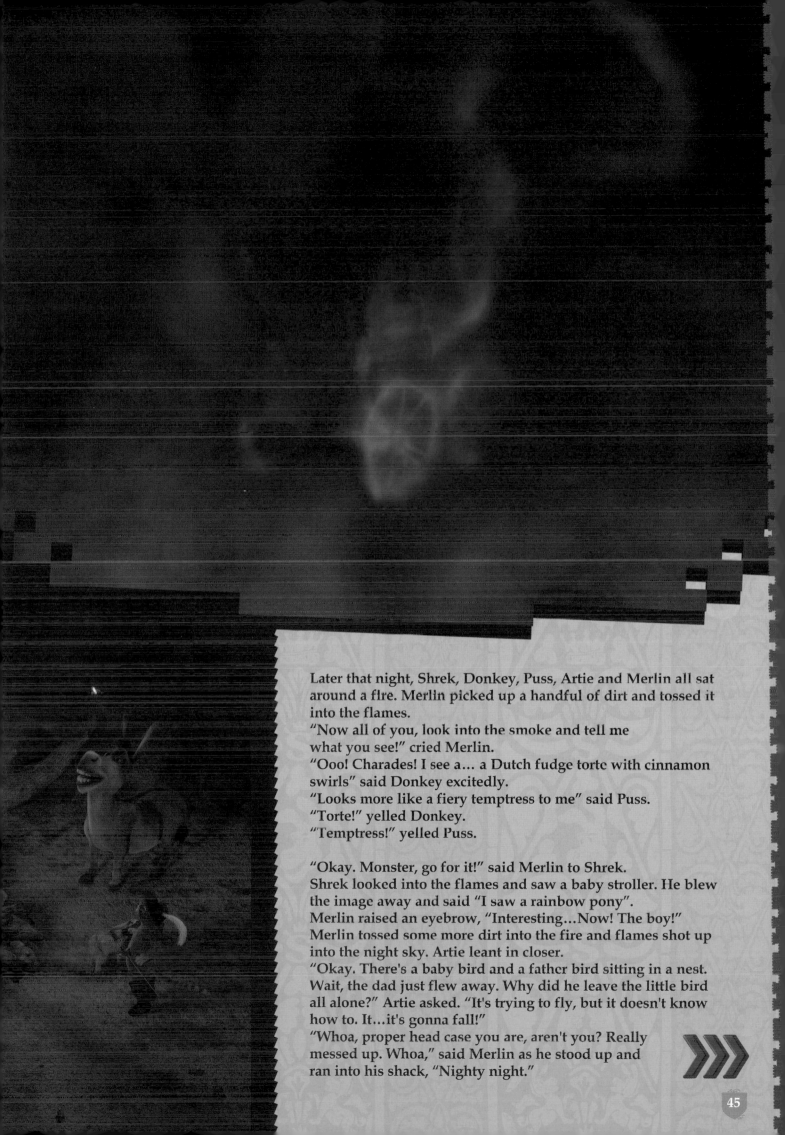

Later that night, Shrek, Donkey, Puss, Artie and Merlin all sat around a fire. Merlin picked up a handful of dirt and tossed it into the flames.

"Now all of you, look into the smoke and tell me what you see!" cried Merlin.

"Ooo! Charades! I see a... a Dutch fudge torte with cinnamon swirls" said Donkey excitedly.

"Looks more like a fiery temptress to me" said Puss.

"Torte!" yelled Donkey.

"Temptress!" yelled Puss.

"Okay. Monster, go for it!" said Merlin to Shrek.

Shrek looked into the flames and saw a baby stroller. He blew the image away and said "I saw a rainbow pony".

Merlin raised an eyebrow, "Interesting…Now! The boy!"

Merlin tossed some more dirt into the fire and flames shot up into the night sky. Artie leant in closer.

"Okay. There's a baby bird and a father bird sitting in a nest. Wait, the dad just flew away. Why did he leave the little bird all alone?" Artie asked. "It's trying to fly, but it doesn't know how to. It…it's gonna fall!"

"Whoa, proper head case you are, aren't you? Really messed up. Whoa," said Merlin as he stood up and ran into his shack, "Nighty night."

Shrek walked over to Artie and cleared his throat. "Look, Artie...Um..."

"I know you want me to be king, but I can't. I'm not cut out for it and I never will be, alright?" said Artie. "Even my own dad knew I wasn't worth the trouble. He dumped me at that school the first chance he got and I never heard from him again."

"My dad wasn't really the fatherly type either" said Shrek.

"Well I doubt he was worse than mine" Artie replied.

"Oh yeah?" asked Shrek, "My father was an ogre. He tried to eat me."

"Okay...I guess that's pretty bad" said Artie chuckling to himself, "Did he ever catch you?"

"Yeah, but I was a bit gamey" laughed Shrek. "I know it's hard to believe with my obvious charm and good looks, but people used to think of me as a villain" said Shrek as Artie looked up at him, "And just because people call you a terrible monster, doesn't mean that's what you are."

"You know, you're okay, Shrek" said Artie with a smile, "You just need to do a little less yelling and use a little more soap."

"Thanks Artie," said Shrek as the two of them settled down for the night.

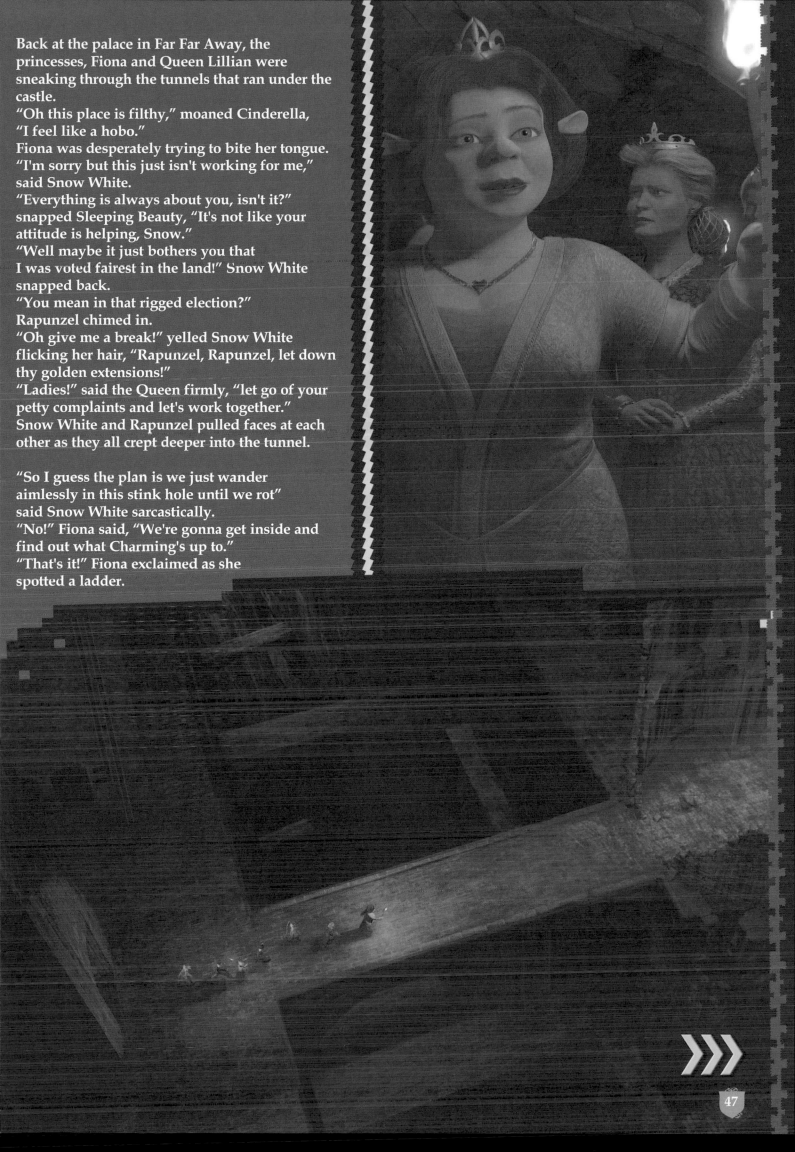

Back at the palace in Far Far Away, the princesses, Fiona and Queen Lillian were sneaking through the tunnels that ran under the castle.

"Oh this place is filthy," moaned Cinderella, "I feel like a hobo."

Fiona was desperately trying to bite her tongue.

"I'm sorry but this just isn't working for me," said Snow White.

"Everything is always about you, isn't it?" snapped Sleeping Beauty, "It's not like your attitude is helping, Snow."

"Well maybe it just bothers you that I was voted fairest in the land!" Snow White snapped back.

"You mean in that rigged election?" Rapunzel chimed in.

"Oh give me a break!" yelled Snow White flicking her hair, "Rapunzel, Rapunzel, let down thy golden extensions!"

"Ladies!" said the Queen firmly, "let go of your petty complaints and let's work together."

Snow White and Rapunzel pulled faces at each other as they all crept deeper into the tunnel.

"So I guess the plan is we just wander aimlessly in this stink hole until we rot" said Snow White sarcastically.

"No!" Fiona said, "We're gonna get inside and find out what Charming's up to."

"That's it!" Fiona exclaimed as she spotted a ladder.

Shrek Quiz

Q1

What is the name of Artie's headmaster at Worcestershire Academy?

A :: **Principal Pynchley**

B :: **Principal Primbottom**

C :: **Principal Poopypants**

Question 2

Can you tell which character from Shrek this is from just looking at their eyes?

A :: **Puss In Boots**

B :: **Pinocchio**

C :: **Donkey**

Q3

How many eyes does Cyclops have?

A :: 1

B :: 2

C :: 3

Q4

What is the name of the king who sadly passed away, forcing Shrek to go and find Artie?

A :: **Harold**

B :: **Charming**

C :: **Farquaad**

Do you love Shrek and all his friends? Do you know everything there is to know about Puss and Donkey? Lets find out! Take this quiz and see if you're a Shrek mega-fan!

Q5

Which one of these is the name of one of Donkey's children?

A :: Pistachio

B :: Peanut

C :: Walnut

Question 6

Who once pulled off Gingerbread Man's legs?

A :: Prince Charming

B :: Captain Hook

C :: Lord Farquaad

Question 7

Who gave Fiona a dwarf at her bridal shower?

A :: Snow White

B :: Rapunzel

C :: Doris

Question 8

Where did Shrek and Donkey first meet?

A :: Far Far Away

B :: Shrek's Swamp

C :: DuLoc

Question 9

What was the name of the page who was caught scratching Shrek's butt?

A :: Fiddlesworth

B :: Piddlesworth

C :: Skiddlesworth

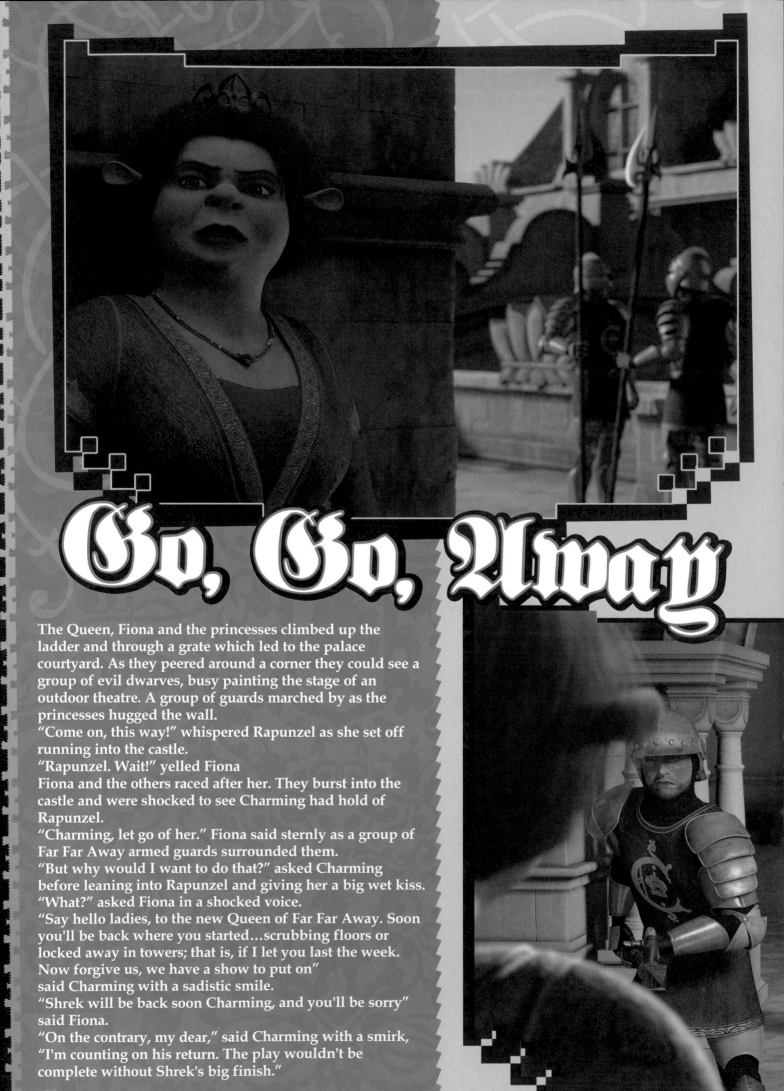

Go, Go, Away

The Queen, Fiona and the princesses climbed up the ladder and through a grate which led to the palace courtyard. As they peered around a corner they could see a group of evil dwarves, busy painting the stage of an outdoor theatre. A group of guards marched by as the princesses hugged the wall.

"Come on, this way!" whispered Rapunzel as she set off running into the castle.

"Rapunzel. Wait!" yelled Fiona

Fiona and the others raced after her. They burst into the castle and were shocked to see Charming had hold of Rapunzel.

"Charming, let go of her." Fiona said sternly as a group of Far Far Away armed guards surrounded them.

"But why would I want to do that?" asked Charming before leaning into Rapunzel and giving her a big wet kiss.

"What?" asked Fiona in a shocked voice.

"Say hello ladies, to the new Queen of Far Far Away. Soon you'll be back where you started...scrubbing floors or locked away in towers; that is, if I let you last the week. Now forgive us, we have a show to put on"
said Charming with a sadistic smile.

"Shrek will be back soon Charming, and you'll be sorry" said Fiona.

"On the contrary, my dear," said Charming with a smirk, "I'm counting on his return. The play wouldn't be complete without Shrek's big finish."

The next morning Shrek woke suddenly at Merlin's shack in the woods. He thought he had heard something but when he looked around, there was no one there. Suddenly the log that Artie was sleeping on sat up, knocking Artie to the floor. The trees came to life and started advancing towards Shrek. From between the trees, Captain Hook appeared, playing the piano!

"Kill 'em all" he yelled, "Except the fat one. King Charming has something special in store for you, ogre."

"King Charming?" Shrek was confused but before he had time to think about it a gang of pirates swung down from the trees and started attacking him.

A group of pirates charged at Donkey, but Puss jumped in front of him and fought off the pirates with his sword. Another pirate ran at Shrek, but Artie tripped him up and the pirate bounced off Shrek's belly.

"Ready the plank!" yelled Captain Hook. Several pirates got a plank and leant it on a tree stump. They forced Shrek on to it, jabbing at him with their swords. Shrek fell backwards into a treasure chest but the pirates couldn't close the lid.

Meanwhile, Puss, Donkey and Artie had been swept up in a net by the evil trees. The pirates produced a cannon and took aim at the three of them. Puss desperately tried to cut through the net as the fuse on the cannon was lit.

"Help!" cried Artie to Shrek.

Ambush

Shrek saw the lit fuse and jumped up but he still had the treasure chest stuck to his butt! He pulled the chest off and stuffed a couple of pirates inside it. Then he threw the chest onto the other end of the plank, which catapulted him high into the air. He landed next to the cannon and had just enough time to spin it around before it fired. The cannonball hurtled towards Captain Hook and hit his piano, blowing it to smithereens.

Realising they had been defeated, the evil trees dropped the net that was holding Puss, Donkey and Artie and ran off. "Cowards!" yelled Captain Hook as the trees and his pirate army ran into the woods.

"What has Charming done with Fiona?" demanded Shrek.

"She's gonna get what's coming to her!" cackled Hook as an evil tree dragged him away, "And there ain't nothing you can do to stop him!"

Merlin's Magic

Shrek, realising that Fiona was in grave danger, set off running towards Far Far Away.

"No, Shrek!" Artie shouted after him, "Hold on a second. I've got an idea."

"Mr. Merlin, they need a spell to get them...I mean, us, back to Far Far Away."

"Forget it," said Merlin, "I don't have that kind of magic in me anymore."

Artie pretended to start crying.

"Oh. What, what's with you?" Merlin asked.

"It's just so hard," Artie sobbed, "You know? They really need to get back 'cause their kingdom's in trouble 'cause there's this really bad man and it's just so hard..."

"Oh, okay..." Merlin conceded, "I'll go and get my things."

Artie turned to Shrek and smiled.

"Now, I am a little rusty, so there may be some side effects," said Merlin.

"Side effects!?" exclaimed Donkey.

"Don't worry, whatever it is or no matter how excruciatingly painful it may be, it'll wear off eventually...I think," continued Merlin.

"On with the whammy zammy," Shrek said, nervously pointing at Merlin.

Merlin started to chant.

"Alacraticious expeditious, a zoomy zoom zoom. Let's help our friends get back, um...soon!"

Magic rays shot from Merlin's fingers and Donkey, Shrek, Puss and Artie disappeared in a puff of smoke!

Follow the Stars!

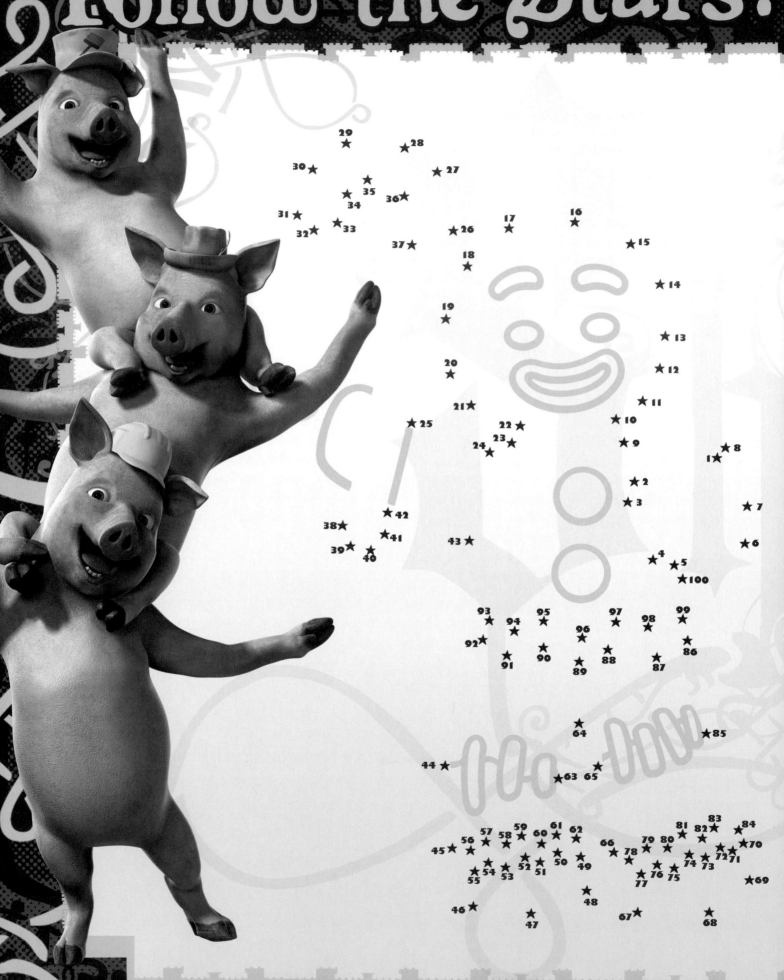

Can you join up all the stars to make two really cool Shrek pictures? Once you have, why not colour them in to make them look extra special?

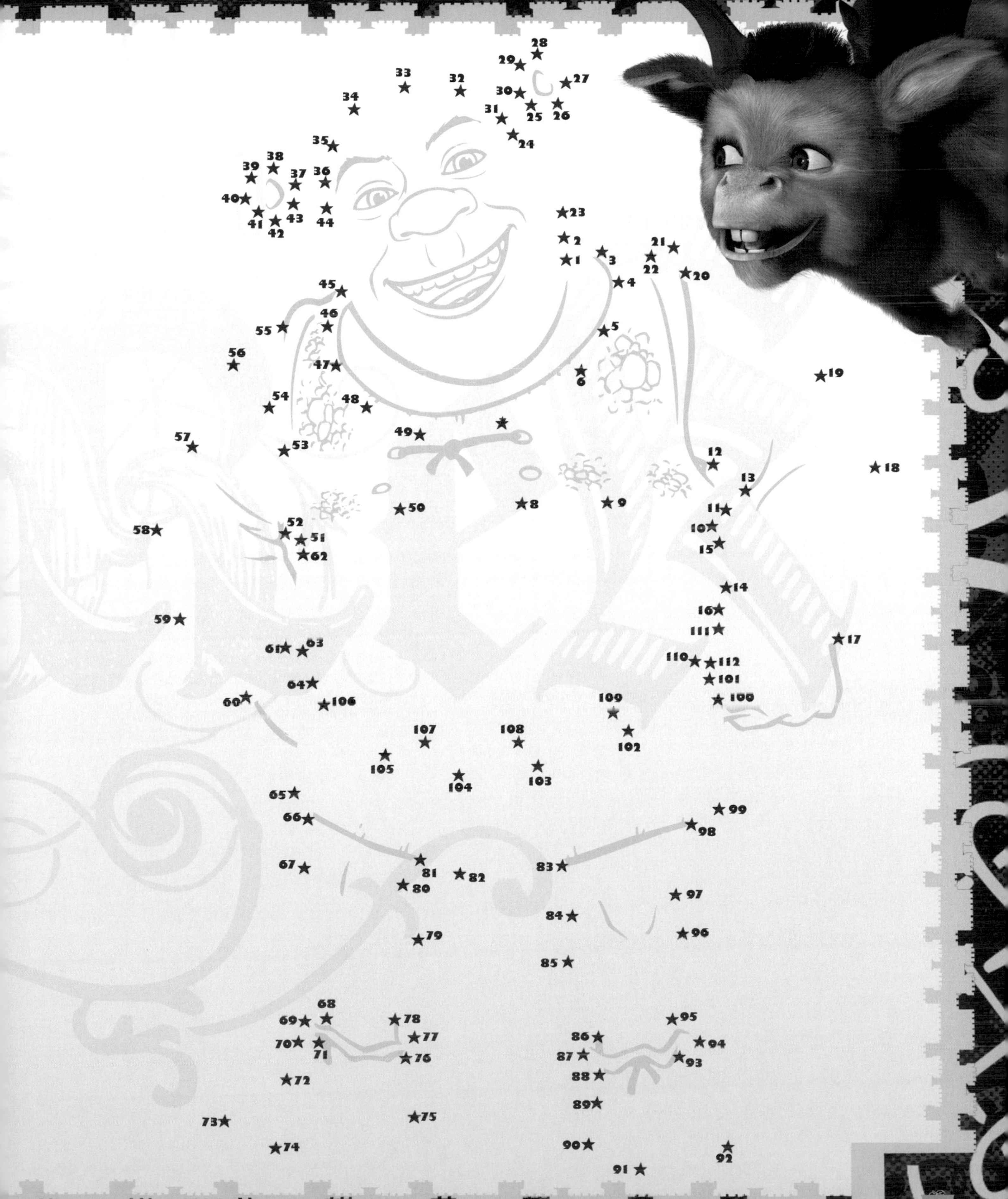

28
29 ★
33 ★ 32 27 ★
34 30 ★
★ 31 ★ 25 26
24
35 ★
38
39 ★ 37 36
40 ★
41 43 44
42
45 ★ 23
46 ★ 2
55 ★ 1 3 21 ★
56 4 22 20
47 ★ 5
54 48 ★ 6
49 ★
57 ★ 53 12
13
52 50 8 9 11
58 ★ 51 10
62 15
59 ★ 14
16
111
61 63 17
64 110 112
60 106 101
109 100
107 108
105 104 103 102
65 ★
66 99
67 ★ 81 82 83 98
80 97
79 84
96
85

68
69 ★ 78
70 77 95
71 86 94
76 87 93
72 88
89
73 ★ 75 90
74 92
91

55

Spot the Difference

Look at these two pictures. They look the same don't they? Actually there are ten little differences. Can you spot them all? Look really carefully, because they are really difficult to spot!

Meet the Characters

SLEEPING BEAUTY

Sleeping Beauty suffers from narcolepsy, an unfortunate condition that leaves her perpetually asleep and a few steps behind. She is a little slow and generally has a hard time following the conversation.

SNOW WHITE

Voted "Fairest In The Land" three times running, Snow White thinks she is the prittiest of the princesses. She has a sarcastic edge and is quick to tell you exactly what she thinks.

MERLIN
Merlin is the high school's former magic teacher. He's an eccentric recluse who has retired to the tranquillity of nature to discover his divine purpose. All he wants is to be left alone in peace. His magic is rusty, and his techniques are extreme, but ultimately he proves to be a helpful resource for Shrek and the boys.

RAPUNZEL
Rapunzel is full of attitude and never afraid to put people in their place. She thinks that she is better than the other princesses and is always using her sharp wit to undermine the other princesses confidence.

CINDERELLA
Obsessive-compulsive and slightly skittish, Cinderella is the most eccentric of the princesses. She is preoccupied with cleanliness and feels out of her element if anything is less than perfect.

Return to Far Far Away

A few moments later, Shrek, Donkey, Puss and Artie reappeared and fell from the sky, close to Far Far Away. They ping-ponged their way down a tree, hitting nearly every branch until they landed in a heap on the floor. Donkey stood up and shook himself.

"Oh man, I haven't been on a trip like that since college!" he said. Only it wasn't Donkey! Well it was, but he was in Puss' body!

"I've been abracadabra'd into a fancy feasting second rate sidekick!" exclaimed Donkey.

"At least you don't look like some kind of bloated roadside piñata," said Puss looking down and realising that he had landed in Donkey's body, "You really should think about going on some kind of diet!"

"Yeah," said Donkey," and you should think about getting yourself a pair of pants! I feel all exposed and nasty."

"I'm really sorry guys," said Artie.

"Don't be!" said Shrek turning to look at Far Far Away which was only a mile or so in front of them, "You got us back kid, thanks."

Shrek, Puss, Donkey and Artie made their way into downtown Far Far Away. They soon came to the sign that used to welcome people to the city but it now read "Go Go Away!"

Inside the Kingdom, there was graffiti everywhere and rubbish covering the streets. Suddenly Shrek noticed something from the corner of his eye.

"Pinocchio?" he asked.

Indeed it was Pinocchio. He was locked in a marionette theatre and being forced to dance for money.

"Help me!" cried the puppet.

"What's happened?" asked a confused Shrek.

"Charming and the villains have taken over everything!" said Pinocchio, "They attacked us but Fiona and the princesses got away. And now she's...."

Before Pinocchio could finish, the curtain on his little glass theatre went down.

"She's what?! She's what!?" cried Shrek, "Puss loan me five bucks!"

Shrek dumped the change into the machine and the curtain went back up. Pinocchio started to dance again.

"Charming's got her locked away in some place secret. You gotta find him! He's probably getting ready for the showwww..." The curtain went down again before Pinocchio could finish.

"Wait, wait, wait!" cried Shrek, "Pinocchio! What show?"

Pinocchio stuck out his hand from under the curtain and pointed to a poster on the wall.

"It's A Happily Ever After, After All!" said Puss reading the poster.

"It's the Ogre! Get him!" yelled a guard.

Shrek turned to see a large group of Prince Charming's royal knights, armed and ready to fight. Artie jumped forward.

"Look don't you know who he thinks he is?" asked Artie to the guards, "How dare you?"

Shrek, picking up on Arties plan, joined in.

"I don't know who dropped the ball on this one, but the carriage was supposed to pick me up at my hotel. Donkey, we're dealing with amateurs."

The guards looked at each other in confusion. They were not sure what was going on.

Artie ripped the poster off the wall and shoved it in their faces.

"He's a star people! Hello?! You can't treat a star like this!" Artie ranted at them, "I'm so sorry Mr. Shrek."

"Just take care of it. And quickly." Shrek snapped.

"I assume you have everything ready for tonight?" Artie asked the guards, "You did get the list for the dressing room, didn't you?"

"I don't think that's our department" answered one of the guards.

"Maybe they should talk to Nancy in Human Resources?" suggested another.

Shrek pushed the confused guards to one side and continued towards the castle.

"Looks like we're gonna have to inform Charming he's got a couple of boobs running the operation," snapped Donkey as the guards looked at each other nervously.

Artie's Answer

Do you know where Artie's least favourite place in the world is? Break the code to find out!

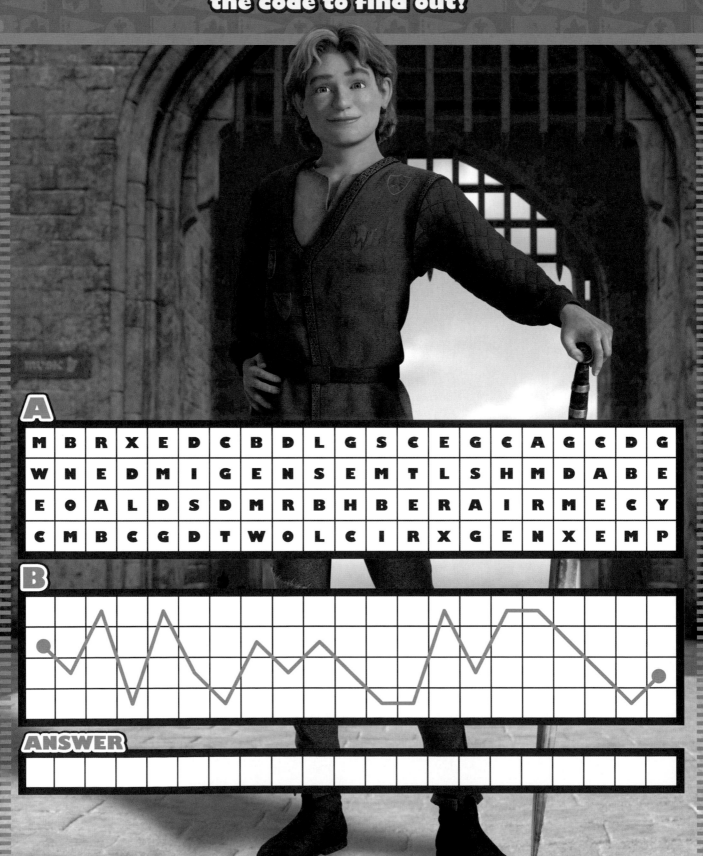

A

M	B	R	X	E	D	C	B	D	L	G	S	C	E	G	C	A	G	C	D	G
W	N	E	D	M	I	G	E	N	S	E	M	T	L	S	H	M	D	A	B	E
E	O	A	L	D	S	D	M	R	B	H	B	E	R	A	I	R	M	E	C	Y
C	M	B	C	G	D	T	W	O	L	C	I	R	X	G	E	N	X	E	M	P

B

ANSWER

The Princesses Puzzle

Fiona and the princesses have to save Shrek from Charming's terrible performance in the theatre. Can you help them find the right route in time?

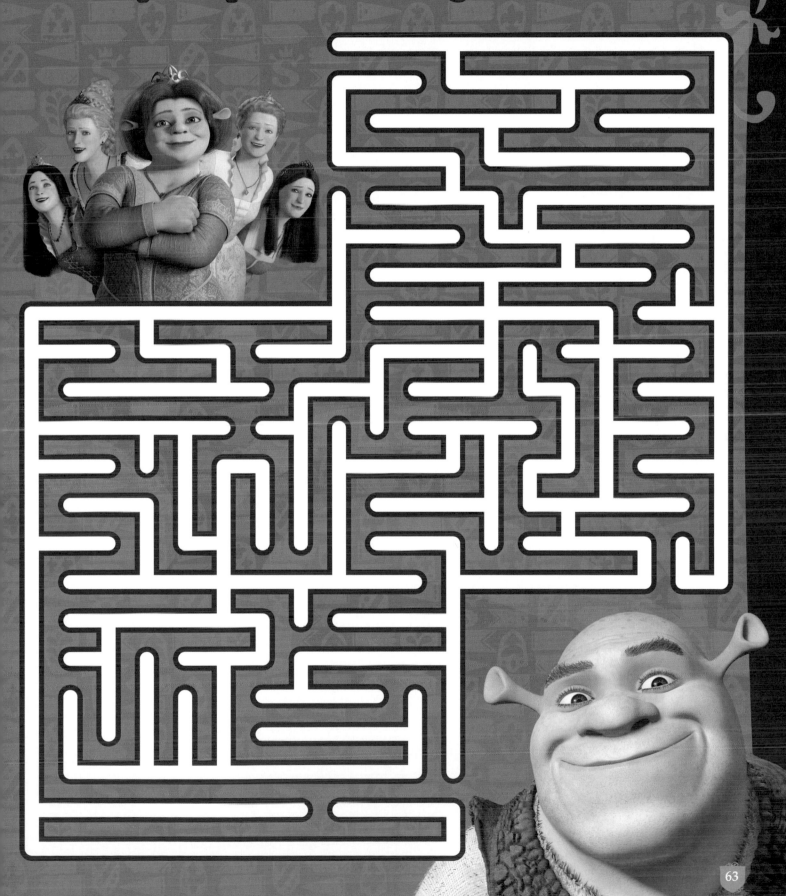

Charming flung open the door to his dressing room and sat down in front of a huge mirror. He looked at himself vainly, admiring his good looks. Then he noticed the reflection of Shrek, Artie, Donkey and Puss standing behind him.

"Break a leg." Shrek growled, "Or, on second thought, let me break it for you."

Shrek approached Charming and backed him into his dresser. Charming fumbled around and pressed a button on the dresser.

"Thank goodness you're here," Charming said, "I was beginning to think you might not make it back…in time."

"Where's Fiona?" Shrek demanded, grabbing Charming by his shirt.

"Don't worry" said Charming slyly, "She and the others are safe. For now."

Suddenly a group of guards burst into the room and quickly surrounded Shrek, Artie, Donkey and Puss.

Charming smiled as Shrek realised he was beaten. He dropped Charming to the floor with a thud.

Charming walked over to Artie.

"Let me guess….Arthur?" asked Charming.

"It's Artie, actually" Artie replied.

"This boy is supposed to be the new king of Far Far Away?" asked Charming as he menacingly held a sword to Artie's throat. "How pathetic."

"That's enough Charming" said Shrek, stepping in. "I'm here now, you got what you wanted. This isn't about him."

Artie stared at Shrek with a
confused look on his face.
"Then who's it about? I'm supposed
to be king, right?" he asked.
Shrek hesitated.
"You weren't really next in line for
the throne...I was. Okay?"
"But you said the king asked for
me personally," said Artie.
"Look!" said Shrek become more
and more defensive, "I said
whatever I had to say, alright!"
Artie was stunned.
"I wasn't right for the job, I just
needed some fool to replace me,
and you fit the bill. So just go!"
Shrek shouted.
"You were just playing me the
entire time?" asked Artie.
"You catch on real fast kid."
Shrek snapped.

Artie looked over at Puss and
Donkey, but they turned away.
"You know, for a minute there, I
actually thought..." started Artie.
"What? That he cared about you?"
interrupted Charming, "He's an
ogre. What did you expect?"
As Charming signalled the guards,
Artie took one last look at Shrek
and then ran out of the room.
"You really do have a way with
children, Shrek," laughed
Charming as the guards
led Shrek away.

65

Princess Power

All the princesses, the Queen and Fiona were all locked up in the same prison cell. Suddenly the cell door flew open and Donkey and Puss were pushed inside.

"Hey, hey, hey, hey" yelled Puss who was still trapped in Donkey's body.

"Yeah, and I have your badge number, "Tin Can…"

"Donkey!?" cried Fiona.

"Fiona" cried Donkey but from inside Puss's body.

"Puss?" asked Fiona looking very confused.

"Lo siento, Princessa, but I am Puss, stuck here inside the hideous body!" said Puss.

"And I'm me!" yelled Donkey.

"But you're…" said Fiona, still totally confused.

"I know, I know" explained Donkey, "Everything's a little fruity in the loops right now. But what happened is, we went to high school, the boat crashed, and we got "bippity-bopity-booped" by the "Magic Man."

"I don't get it" said Cinderella.

"The cat turned into a little horse that smells like feet. What's to get?" asked Snow White.

"Where's Shrek?" asked Fiona.
"Charming's got him," said Donkey, "And he plans on killing Shrek tonight in front of the whole Kingdom."
"Alright everyone, we need to find a way out, now!" said Fiona.
The princesses nodded in agreement.
"You're right!" said Snow White, "Ladies, assume the position!"
Sleeping Beauty fell asleep standing up. Snow White lay down and puckered her lips. Cinderella dusted off a spot on the bench and sat down with her legs crossed.

"What are you doing?" asked Fiona.
"Waiting to be rescued," replied Sleeping Beauty.
"You have got to be kidding me!" said Fiona desperately.
"Well what do you expect us to do? We're just three super hot princesses, two circus freaks, a pregnant ogre and an old lady."

" Hmm. Excuse me!" said the Queen, "Old lady coming through."
The Queen walked straight up to the wall of the prison cell and let out a piercing "Hiiiyyyiiiaaaah!" as she head butted a hole straight through!
All the princesses couldn't believe what they had just seen.
"Mom!?" said Fiona in a shocked voice.
"Well, you didn't actually think you got your fighting skills from your father, did you?" the Queen asked her daughter.

Shrek A-Z

 A is for Artie, the heir to the throne of Far Far Away.

 B is for The Three Blind Mice, who sometimes nibble on Shrek's ear.

 C is for Cinderella, one of the princesses who uses her glass slipper as a weapon!

 D is for Donkey, Shrek's best buddy.

 E is for Evil Tree, although in the end, the trees aren't evil at all!

 F is for Fiona, the love of Shrek's life.

 G is for Gingy, who is one tough cookie!

 H is for Harold who sadly passed away, or you might say he croaked!

 I is for In Love. Shrek and Fiona are so in love that they are going to start a family.

J is for Jousting, one of the top sports at Worcester Academy.

 K is for King. Shrek really doesn't want to be king, but Charming does!

 L is for Lillian. Lillian is the Queen of Far Far Away.

 M is for Merlin. Merlin's magic might be a bit rusty but he really came through for Shrek and the gang!

 N is for Nanny. Snow White gave Fiona a nanny dwarf at her baby shower.

 O is for Ogre. Ogre's aren't as mean as they look you know!

 P is for Puss In Boots, the bravest kitty cat in all the land!

 Q is for Queen. One day Artie will have to find a Queen, perhaps Guinevere would like the job?

 R is for Rapunzel, whose golden locks turned out to be nothing more than a wig!

 S is for Shrek, who looks green on the outside, but has a heart of gold.

 T is for Three Little Pigs, who if they keep stuffing their faces like they do, won't be little much longer!

 U is for Ugly. Some people call Doris ugly, I don't know why!

 V is for Vermin Filled. Shrek loves his vermin filled swamp and can't wait to get back to it.

 W is for the Big Bad Wolf, who isn't really all that bad!

 X is for Xenophobic which is a posh word that means you don't like someone for no reason, just like how Charming feels about Shrek.

 Y is for Yucky, which is how an Swamp Shake must taste!

 Z is for Zap. Merlin zapped the gang with his magic and got them back to Far Far Away!

Dronkeys to Donkey

Can you work out which of the Dronkeys are on the right path to find their dad, Donkey?

A

B

C

Follow The Arrows

Follow the arrows around the grid and see which of Shrek's buddies he will meet up with.

Fiona beamed at her mother and turned to the princesses.

"Okay girls, from here on out, we're going to take care of business ourselves," said Fiona firmly.

The princesses all stared at her intently.

"So, why didn't she just bust through the wall earlier?" asked Snow White.

"Do you want your happily ever after back, or not?" replied Fiona. Snow White thought about it for a moment before glancing over at the other princesses and nodding. Then she got a determined look on her face and ripped off a sleeve from her dress, revealing a tattoo. Sleeping Beauty ripped off the hem of her dress while the Queen took out her lipstick and painted war paint on her face. Cinderella hurriedly sharpened the heel of her glass slipper. All the women placed their hands in a circle. They were ready to fight!

Fox Force Five

In another part of the city, Charming's show was about to begin. Captain Hook unscrewed his hook and replaced it with a conductor's baton.

"Ladies and gentlemen," the announcer's voice boomed throughout the theatre, "The Far Far Away Theatre at the Charming Pavilion is proud to present: "It's a Happily Ever After, After All."

Two intimidating looking knights were handing out programs and ushering people into their seats with their spears.

"Enjoy your evening of theatrical reverie, citizen! Oy! No food or beverages in the theatre!" they shouted.

The orchestra began to warm up as Shrek waited below the stage, looking like a beaten man.

Cyclops was tying up his arms and legs with heavy chains to the floor.

"Oww. Easy" moaned Shrek as
Cyclops tightened the chains.
"Sorry. I guess I was just showing off
for the little one," said Cyclops
"Huh?" asked Shrek.
"It's "Bring your kids to work day."
C'mere beautiful." Cyclops said as he
motioned into the shadows.
From the shadows emerged Cyclops'
daughter. She looked just like him,
except she had long hair a was
wearing a dress.
"Well..." said Shrek
"she's got your eye."
"Who woulda thought a monster like
me deserves something as special as
you?" Cyclops asked his daughter
and he picked her up for a cuddle.
Shrek began to think about Fiona and
their baby and a determined look
came across his face.

Outside the castle walls, Fiona and the princesses hid. Two evil trees were guarding the castle gates. Fiona let out a duck call to signal Snow White. Snow skipped down the garden path towards The evil trees, singing to herself.

As she sung, the birds in the garden answered her. "Little birdies take wing, flitting down from the trees they appear, and to chirp in my ear," she sang. All the forest creatures flocked to her.

"All because I sing. Ahh ha ha ha ha haaa," Snow sang.

Even more animals flocked to her as the evil trees stared on in amazement.

Suddenly, Snow Whites face changed. She looked incredibly angry and the beautiful song she was singing, became sinister.

All the forest animals charged at the evil trees and attacked them. Fiona and the princesses charged towards the castle gates.

"Move it! Go! Go! Go!" yelled Fiona.

Meanwhile, Donkey and Puss ran into Far Far Away Zoo where the Dronkeys were being held captive in a cage. Donkey busted the door open and the Dronkeys flew out.

"My babies" cried Donkey.

But the Dronkeys flew over to Puss and hugged him. They didn't know that Puss and Donkey had swapped bodies!

Then, they freed Gingy and Pinocchio and the rest of the Far Far Away friends.

The princesses ran towards the castle gates.
Doris punched through the lock to let them in. As they approached a group of guards, Cinderella grabbed her glass slipper and threw it at them. It acted like a boomerang and flew through the air knocked two of the guards out cold!
Sleeping Beauty fell down asleep and a couple more guards tripped over her and went flying through the air. Doris ran over to a wall and took a knee. She boosted the princesses, Fiona and the Queen, up and over the wall. Donkey, Puss and the fairy-tale friends ran towards the castle.
Donkey turned to the creatures behind him and said "All right people, let's do this thing! Go

Team Dy-No-Mite!!"
"I thought we had agreed we
would go by the name of
Team Super Cool,"
complained Pinocchio.
"As I recall it was Team
Awesome," Gingerbread Man
chimed in.
"I voted for Team Alpha Wolf
Squadron" said Wolf.
"Alright! Alright! Alright!"
said Donkey, "From
henceforth we are to be known
as Team Alpha Super
Awesome Cool Dynomite
Wolf Squadron."

One of the three pigs noticed
something in the shadows.
"Ach to Lieber!" he said,
"There is some strange little
girl over there staring at us!"
Donkey turned to look.
It was Artie.

"Artie!" yelled Donkey, but Artie just turned and walked away. Puss ran over to him.

"Wait, wait, wait, wait, wait. Hey! Where is the fire, Senor?" asked Puss.

Artie pushed Puss out of his way.

"Oh please, don't act so innocent. You both knew what was going on the whole time and you kept it to yourself," accused Artie.

"Artie," cried Donkey, "it's not like it seems."

"Oh really? Because it seemed like a set up from the start. He never believed in me," said Artie.

"Come on, didn't Shrek teach you anything? Don't believe everything everyone says about you," said Donkey.

"Si, he only said those things to protect you!" added Puss.

"Shrek saved your life," said Donkey gently.

Artie was stunned by what Donkey had said, but it all suddenly made sense. Shrek hadn't meant what he had said in Charming's dressing room, he had only said it to get Artie out of danger.

The Final Showdown

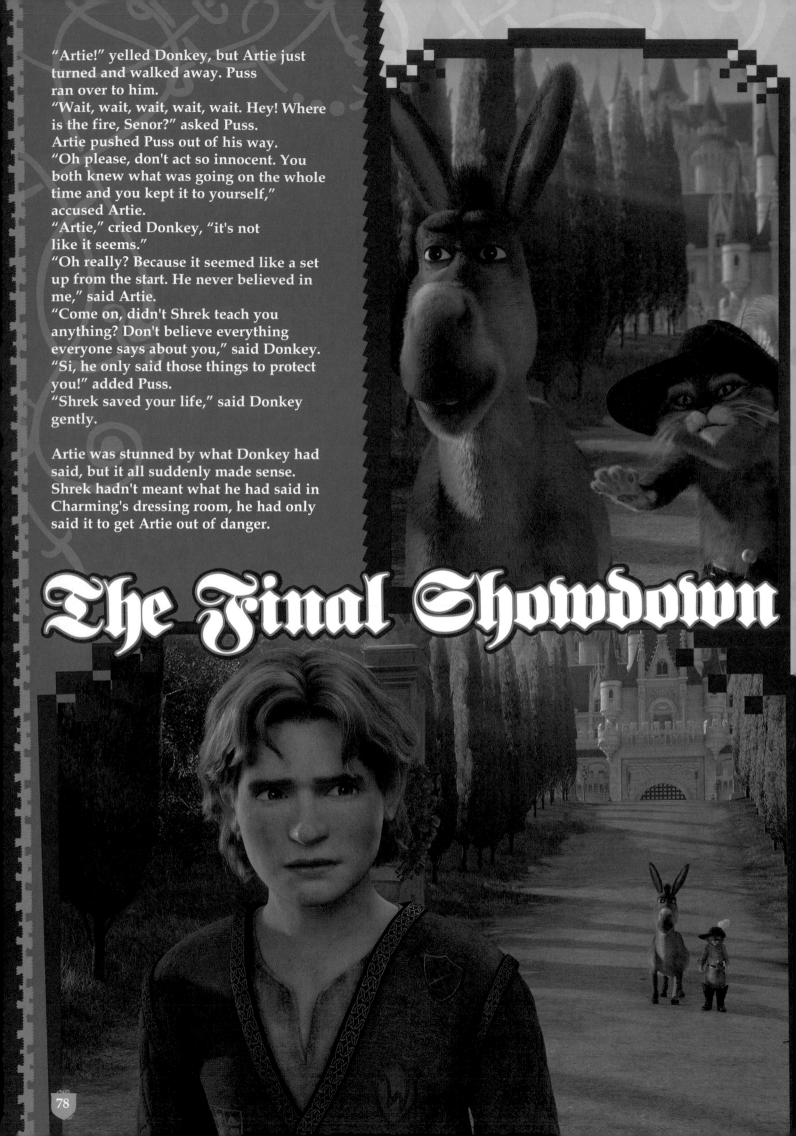

Back at the theatre, the show was underway. "Cue the spot!" ordered Rumpelstiltskin.
A spotlight shone upon Rapunzel who was in a tower onstage. She began to sing;
"I wait alone up here.
I'm trapped another day.
Locked up here - please set me free.
My new life I almost see,
A castle, you and me.
Yes, a castle you and me…"

Nearby, a clamshell opened and revealed Prince Charming on horseback.

"Tis I! Tis I!
Upon my noble steed!
Princess, my love,
At last you will be freed!" sang Charming.

Perfect Pairs

We all know that Shrek and Fiona are the perfect couple. Just look at how happy they look in all these pictures. Can you match the picture to the frames and make the perfect pairs?

ANSWERS: A:: _ B:: _ C:: _ D:: _ E:: _ F:: _ G:: _

Prince Charming rode over to the tower in which Rapunzel was waiting.
"Through the blistering desert,
Across the stormiest sea,
Facing creatures so vile,
So you can gaze upon me!"
sang Charming as he made his way up the stairs of the tower.

"I knew you'd come for me.
And now we finally meet," sang Rapunzel.
"I knew you'd wait.
And from my plate of love you'd eat,"
Charming sang back.

Some of the audience looked at each other, thinking to themselves 'Is this for real?' Rapunzel let down her hair and Charming started towards it but as he did a loud flash and a sinister growling boomed throughout the auditorium. Charming hammed it up for the audience, placing his hand to his ear.

A large imposing swamp shack rose onto the stage. In front of it stood a shackled Shrek. He pulled at his chains trying to escape, but it was to no avail.

"Who is this ugly fiend who so rudely intervened?" sang Charming, staring at Shrek.

A chorus line of pirates and evil knights danced onto the stage from the wings.

"Will Charming fight? Or will he flee?"
they sang in harmony.

"Oh please, rescue me!" sang Rapunzel.

"From this monstrosity!" sang the chorus line.

"Fear thee not Honey Lamb!
I will slice this thing up like a HAM!" sang Charming.

"Oh boy," muttered Shrek.

Prince Charming pulled out his sword and relished the moment for a while.

"You are about to enter
a world of pain with which you are not....
FamiliaAAAAAR!"

The last note was so high, and
Charming held it for so long that some of the
audiences glasses shattered!

"Well it can't be anymore painful than the lousy performance you're giving," chuckled Shrek.

The audience burst out laughing. Prince Charming was a little thrown by their reaction.

Rumplestiltskin had to feed Charming his next line, "Prepare foul beast," he whispered.

Charming composed himself.

"Prepare foul beast, your time is done," sang Charming a little off key.

"Oooh, if you don't mind could you kill me, and then sing," Shrek mocked.

Prince Charming got right up in Shrek's face.

"Be quiet!" Charming growled.

"Oh come on, I'm just havin' fun with ya. That's actually a very nice leotard," said Shrek

"Thank you," said Charming

"Do they come in men's sizes?" asked Shrek.

The audience burst in to laughter again! Shrek smiled, enjoying how he was messing up the show. Prince Charming on the other hand was furious.

"Enough!" yelled Charming. The audience fell silent.

"Now you'll know what it's like to have everything you've worked for, everything that's precious to you taken away!" he screamed at Shrek. Prince Charming raised his sword, "Now you'll know how I felt!" he yelled.

Just as Charming was bout to strike down Shrek, a fireball flew across the stage, hitting his sword and melting it.

"Ahhhh!" cried Charming.

It was Dragon! She flew above the theatre with the Dronkeys. Then, the Three Pigs jumped onto the stage and struck a fighting pose. Pinocchio followed them, landing on stage with a flurry of kung-fu moves. Gingerbread Man popped up inside Rapunzel's tower. He grabbed her hair and swung down but before he reached the floor, Rapunzel's hair came away from her head, revealing that it was a wig all along! Rapunzel screamed and ran off stage crying.

Charming looked around in surprise. Suddenly a huge shadow fell across the crowd, making them gasp. Dragon and the Dronkeys landed on the stage and Puss and Donkey jumped off her back!

"Pray for mercy from..." yelled Donkey.

"...Puss!" cried Puss.

"And Donkey!" yelled Donkey.

Finally Queen Lillian head butted her way through the set, followed by Sleeping Beauty and Doris. Snow White flew in behind them like a ninja, with help from her woodland creatures. And Cinderella ran on stage with a mop as her chosen weapon. Together, all the princesses struck fierce fighting poses and stood next to Shrek.

With a bang, the front door of the swamp house crashed to the floor revealing Fiona!

"He honey!" she yelled to Shrek, "Sorry we're late. You okay?"

"Much better, now that you're here!" said Shrek as the two embraced.

The audience broke out into applause. Shrek turned to Prince Charming and raised his shackled wrists.

"So Charming, you wanna let me out these so we can settle this ogre to man?" he asked. "Oooh, that sounds fun. But I have a better idea!" replied Charming. He clapped his hands and Cyclops emerged from a trap door in the stage, knocking Puss and Donkey over. The witches flew onto the stage and threatened the princesses with their broomsticks. Gingerbread Man was suddenly surrounded by the evil knights and the evil dwarves grabbed The Three Pigs. An evil tree grabbed the wolf and held him tightly, while Mable held an axe to Pinocchio. Dragon was about to help but she found herself surrounded by knights with crossbows. Then, a bunch of pirates grabbed Fiona and tied her up!

"Fiona!' cried Shrek, but it was too late. "Let go of me!" yelled Fiona trying to free herself from the pirates.

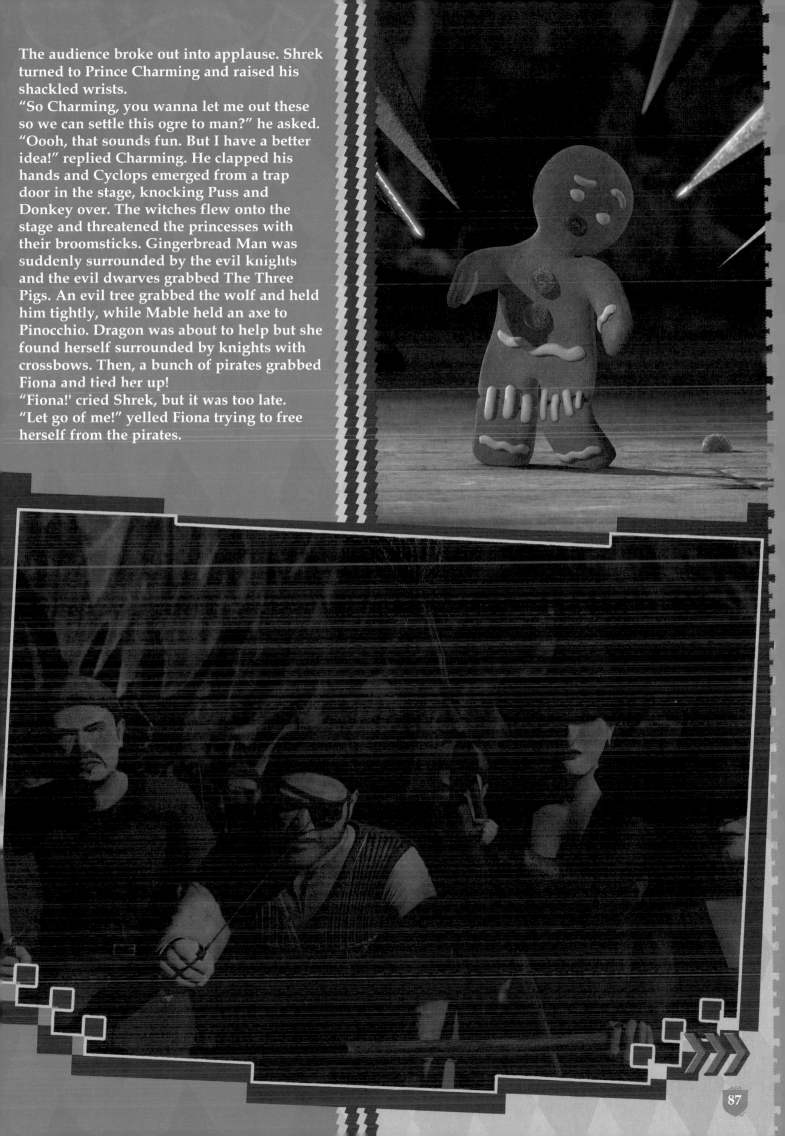

Prince Charming's eyes narrowed. He reached out and took the Headless Horseman's sword from him. He smiled as he stepped towards Shrek.

"You will not ruin things this time" Charming said menacingly, "This is my Happily Ever After!"

Charming raised his sword and was about to strike when a bright spotlight suddenly glared in his face.

"Hold it!" a voice yelled.

Everyone turned to see Artie.

"Oh, what is it now?" cried Charming in an exasperated voice.

Artie jumped down from the spotlight and landed on stage between Shrek and the villains.

"Ooooohh!" cried the audience, unsure whether this was part of the show or not.

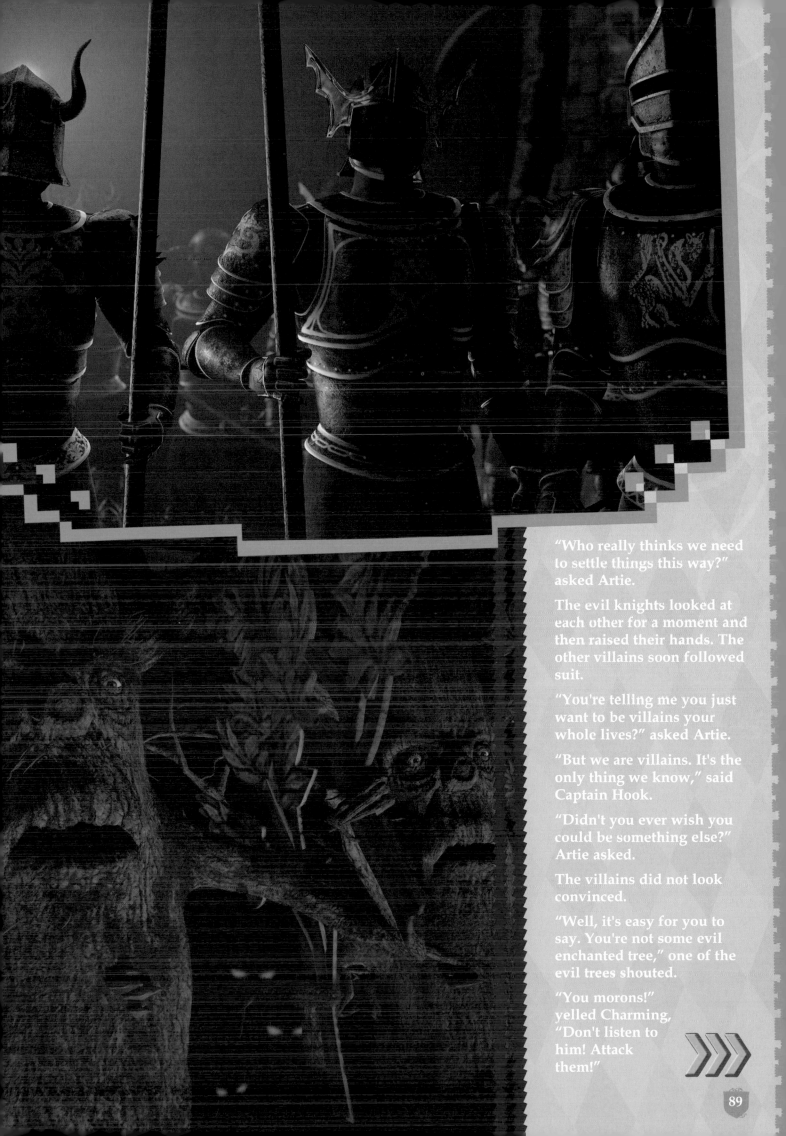

"Who really thinks we need to settle things this way?" asked Artie.

The evil knights looked at each other for a moment and then raised their hands. The other villains soon followed suit.

"You're telling me you just want to be villains your whole lives?" asked Artie.

"But we are villains. It's the only thing we know," said Captain Hook.

"Didn't you ever wish you could be something else?" Artie asked.

The villains did not look convinced.

"Well, it's easy for you to say. You're not some evil enchanted tree," one of the evil trees shouted.

"You morons!" yelled Charming, "Don't listen to him! Attack them!"

Meet the Characters

GINGERBREAD MAN
Gingy may look soft and sweet, but in fact he is one tough cookie! When the chocolate chips are down, he's ginger-bred to be a sweet friend how can always be relied on.

PINNOCCHIO
To caring, sharing Pinocchio, honesty is very important. If he tells a fib, his nose grows as long as a flagpole and gives him away! He is a carved puppet who longs to be a real boy. He may be made of wood but his loving kind heart is anything but wooden.

THE THREE LITTLE PIGS
Shrek used to find the pigs and their squealing grating. But when you are being pursued by a rabble of rogues, you have to take help where you can find it.

THE THREE BLIND MICE
Among the smallest of the magical fairy-tale creatures that live in Shrek's swamp are the Three Blind Mice. The Three Blind Mice are always bumping into things and occasionally nibble on Shrek's ear, mistaking it for a piece of cheese!

THE BIG BAD WOLF
An old-fashioned wolf, he sticks to the tricks he knows: dress up like an old woman and blow down pig's houses before they master the art of cement-mixing.

DRAGON

Charged with guarding Princess Fiona within her castle prison, Dragon lived a lonely life. That was until she met Donkey and the unlikely pair fell in love. Dragon might be fiery but she is also tender-hearted.

DRONKEYS

Dragon and Donkey are proud parents to five little fire-breathing dronkeys. But as with all little ones they sometimes need a bit of guidance. What parent hasn't had to tell their son to stop roasting marshmallows on his sister's head!

Picture Perfect Princesses

Can you work out which of these pictures is which princess? Write their names in the space on the picture frame.

1)

2)

3)

4)

5)

PRINCESS FIONA

SLEEPING BEAUTY

CINDERELLA

RAPUNZEL

SNOW WHITE

Hail King Artie

Another of the evil trees grabbed Prince Charming and covered his mouth.
"What Steve's trying to say here is that it's hard to come by honest work when the whole world is against you," the tree said to Artie.
"Okay, fair enough," said Artie, "You're right. I'm not a talking tree. But a good friend of mine once told me just because people treat you like a villain doesn't mean you are one…"
The fairy-tale villains listened intently to what Artie had to say.
"The thing that matters most is what you think of yourself," continued Artie, "If there's something you really want to be, then the only person standing in your way is you."

"I've always wanted to learn guitar," said the Headless Horseman.
"I'd like to open up a Spa in France," said the Evil Queen.

The villains looked thoughtfully at their weapons. Suddenly the pirates threw down their swords, followed by the evil knights and the witches. They all cheered and started introducing themselves to the fairy-tale friends. The pirates untied Fiona and Gingerbread Man shook hands with an evil knight.

Suddenly, Prince Charming broke free of the evil tree's grip and charged. He grabbed a sword from the discarded pile and raised it in the air, his aim firmly set on Artie. Just as he was about to strike the young heir, Shrek summoned the strength to break free of his chains. He managed to lasso Charming's sword with one of the chains and pull Charming away from Artie. Furious, Charming charged at Shrek, desperately stabbing at him with the sword. With a grunt Shrek fell to the floor.

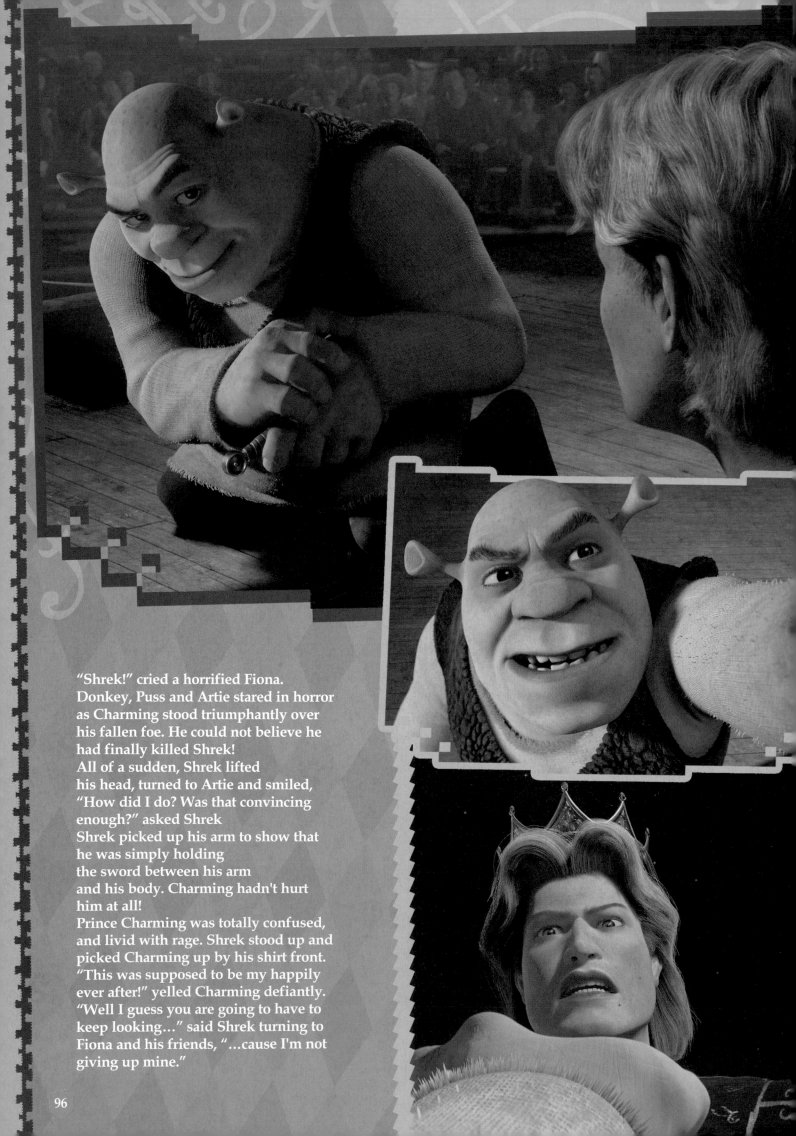

"Shrek!" cried a horrified Fiona.
Donkey, Puss and Artie stared in horror
as Charming stood triumphantly over
his fallen foe. He could not believe he
had finally killed Shrek!
All of a sudden, Shrek lifted
his head, turned to Artie and smiled,
"How did I do? Was that convincing
enough?" asked Shrek
Shrek picked up his arm to show that
he was simply holding
the sword between his arm
and his body. Charming hadn't hurt
him at all!
Prince Charming was totally confused,
and livid with rage. Shrek stood up and
picked Charming up by his shirt front.
"This was supposed to be my happily
ever after!" yelled Charming defiantly.
"Well I guess you are going to have to
keep looking…" said Shrek turning to
Fiona and his friends, "…cause I'm not
giving up mine."

Shrek dropped Charming to the floor and signalled to Dragon. She casually tipped over the tower with her tail which landed on Charming and trapped him inside.

"Mommy!" cried Charming as the tower came crashing down.

Shrek turned to Fiona and they smiled at each other. As the dust settled on the stage, the Royal Crown rolled across the floor. Artie bent down to pick it up.

"It's yours if you want it," said Shrek to Artie.

Artie starred at the crown, unsure of what he should do.

"You've got what it takes kid," encouraged Shrek, "Don't let anybody ever tell you otherwise."

Artie turned to the crowd, they all began
to cheer him. Artie lifted the crown high
into the air and paced it on his head.
The crowd in the theatre went crazy.
People were hoopin' and hollerin' and
cheering as loudly as they could.
Shrek stepped forwards and draped his
arm around Artie's shoulders.
"Ar-tie! Ar-tie! Ar-tie! Ar-tie!"
the crowd cheered.

In a puff of smoke, Merlin suddenly appeared. He looked around a little confused, clutching at his show ticket. "Excuse me, that's my seat," he said to no one in particular. Suddenly he was dragged onto the stage by Donkey and Puss.

"Okay, senor hocus-y pocus-y. The time has come to rectify some wrongs!" said Puss from Donkey's body.
"Cause I'm not doing anymore of these 'cat baths'" yelled Donkey.
"Please say you didn't!" begged Puss staring at Donkey with a disgusted look on his face.

"Now let's do this thing!" Puss demanded turning his attention to Merlin.

"Uh...alright, alright...uh" Merlin stammered.

Merlin rubbed his hands together vigorously.

"You're going to feel a little pinch, and possibly some lower intestinal discomfort, but this should do the trick," said Merlin.

Puss and Donkey looked at each other nervously.

Merlin rolled up his long baggy sleeves and let loose with a bright burst of magical light which enveloped Puss and Donkey.

It took Puss and Donkey a few moments to recover from the magical blast they had just received and when they had pulled themselves together, they looked at each other for a few seconds.

"Are you...?" asked Puss.

Donkey lifted up his hoof and inspected it carefully.

"I'm me again!" he yelped joyfully.

Puss checked out his own paws.

"And I'm not you!" he cried, equally as happy as Donkey.

Donkey and Puss gave each other a big, long hug and walked away together laughing.

As Merlin watched he noticed that Donkey still had Puss's tail and Puss still had Donkey's!

"Ooops!" said Merlin as he quietly slipped away.

Shrek walked over to Fiona.

"I'm sorry I left you, I should have never gone," he said lovingly.

"For what it's worth...I think you would have made a great king," said Fiona.

"I have something much more important in mind," Shrek said with a smile as he touched Fiona's belly.

BABY PHOTOS

When Shrek and Fiona had their babies, they only had a black and white camera! Can you add some colour to these baby pictures?

Artie's Anagrams

Artie loves a challenge. Can you help him work out with character names these are?

1. ARK HOLDING

2. SPIN FACE IRONS

3. RING CRANE CHIMP

4. IN ALIEN QUELL

5. CHINA OAK TOP

6. TEN LOCAL

7. SO SNOB SITUP

8. DID ELF THROWS

Who is it?

Look at the pictures below. Can you work out which character is below Donkey, above Merlin and in between Dragon and Shrek?

Answer:

And Babies Make Five!

After everything had settled down in Far Far Away, Shrek and Fiona returned to the peace and quiet of the swamp.

Shrek was busy making an ogre shake out of slug juice, eye balls and worms. He tossed the bottle to Fiona, then walked over to the fire to join her.

"Ah, finally," said a contented Shrek.

Two ogre babies crawled over to Fiona and sat on her lap.

A third ogre baby crawled over to Shrek and he bent down to pick him up.

"Da da!" said the baby.

They were one big happy family of five! Shrek laughed and gave the babies and Fiona a big hug.

"Hey! I smell Shrek junior," came a voice from outside.

The door opened to reveal Donkey and Puss. They both walked into the house with the Dronkeys swarming in behind them. Shrek had a safety pin in his mouth and was busy trying to change diapers, he was now an expert.

Meanwhile, Puss sat down next to one of the ogre babies who had a dummy in his mouth. The baby took the dummy out of his mouth and shoved it into Puss's, giving him a big hug.

Suddenly there was a knock at the door. Shrek went to open it and there stood the nanny dwarf that Snow White had given to Fiona at the baby shower.

"Where's the baby?" the dwarf asked, as Shrek slammed the door in his face. Then Shrek turned back to Fiona and the babies and smiled to himself, this really was a happily ever after, he thought.

The End

Answers

P16

Crossword solution:

```
C Y C L O P S
P I N O C C H I O
      D R O N K E Y        P E N D R A G O
S                  D O N K E Y   M E R L I N
H R E K
K I N G H A R O L D
P R I N C E C H A R M I N G
```

(PRINCESS FION, PRINCE vertical words)

P17

Word search grid:

```
G F G G G Y C O X N Y G L U N
Y A I H I R H Q D D D I I I O F
E S P O Q Q A L X O L L G K W
K Y E K N O R D W L F A R C C
N E C I M A M Q I A R P T E A
O E M P D O I A T D U M B G M
D K P C I P N O V S I D H S S
L H I T C N G S S Z H N Y E G
A Z P H T D O I W F N A G H I
R V G Q I I U C A R S H R E K
T H H N Q T K I C T A A J I P
I S E H I S P C X H P S O M P
E X O B M K U V U X I Z Z D L
T Y S M P S Y R K C K O N R I
B A Z B A Z W J J F S R H C B
```

P36 SHREK LIKES SNOT

P48 1 :: A • 2 :: C • 3 :: A • 4 :: A
5 :: B • 6 :: C • 7 :: A • 8 :: B • 9 :: A

P62 WORCESTERSHIRE ACADEMY

P56

P63

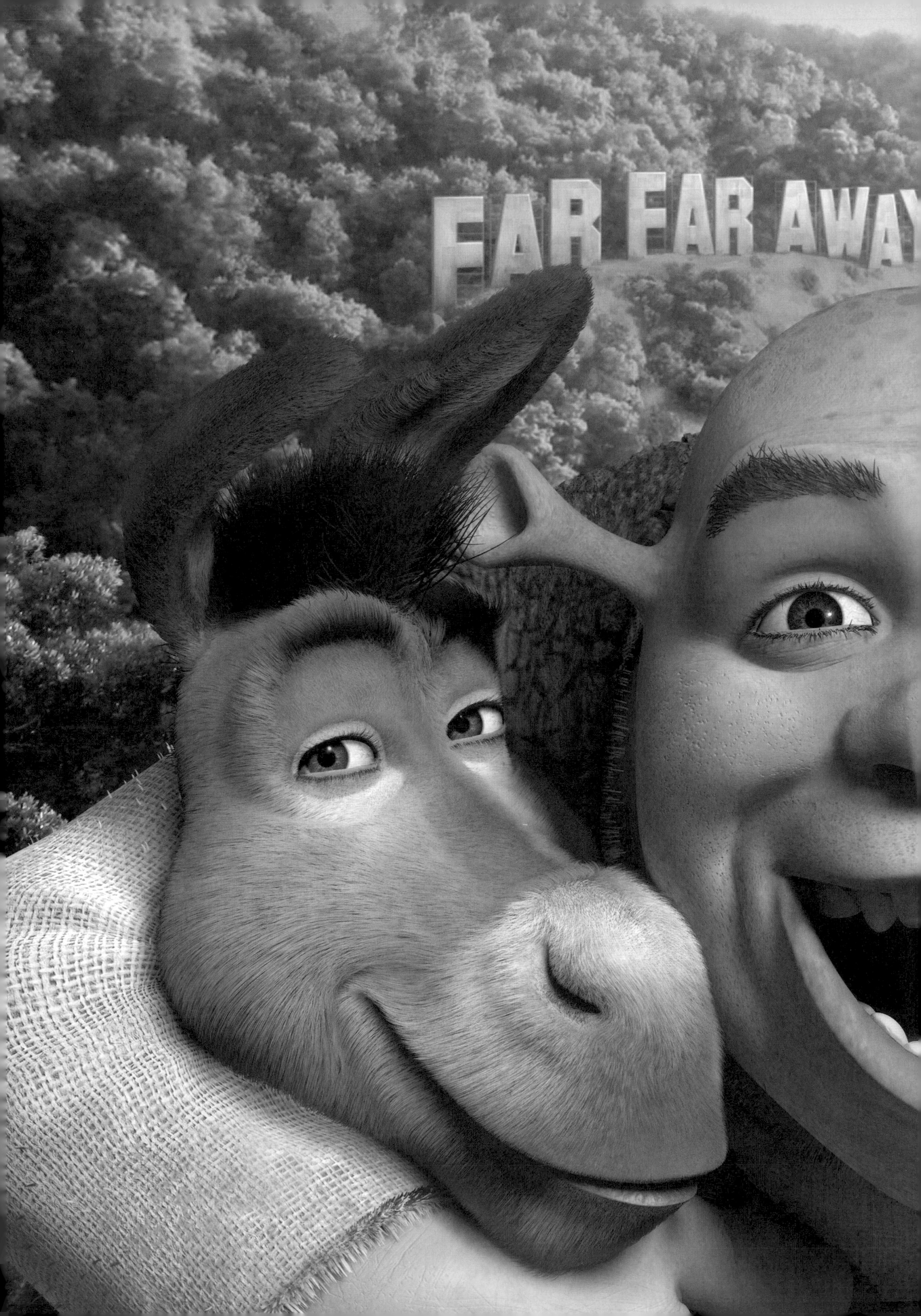
FAR FAR AWAY